GOING
TO POT

GOING TO POT

A practical guide to houseplants
GEOFF HAMILTON

Drawings by Lorna Turpin

BRITISH BROADCASTING CORPORATION

Published by the British Broadcasting Corporation
35 Marylebone High Street, London W1M 4AA

ISBN 0 563 20405 2

First published 1985 © Geoff Hamilton 1985
Printed by Jolly & Barber Ltd, Rugby, Warwickshire

CONTENTS

INTRODUCTION

When we first started to plan a series and a book on houseplants, we asked ourselves, 'What is the most important thing the houseplant grower wants to know?'

We enquired amongst our friends and neighbours and were interested to find that the most common answer was, 'How to keep the darned things alive.' With a few exceptions, most people felt that as soon as a plant was brought into the house it started the slow process of dying. Sometimes it wasn't that slow, either.

Then I discovered several gifted indoor gardeners with fingers green right up to their elbows. They wanted an entirely different kind of information. 'How can I propagate in the cheapest possible way?' 'What can I grow in a corner where there's no light at all?' 'Can I eat the dozen oranges I've grown on the tree in my front room?' We began to feel it might be better if *they* wrote the book!

However, what it did prove to us was this. If you're successful, growing houseplants, like growing anything else, is compulsive. Once you persuade that first geranium to flower, you may as well face the fact that it's going to become a consuming passion. Eventually, your bath will be filled with orchids and you won't be able to find the television for cheese plants. Certainly, most houseplant growers start by wanting to keep their plants alive, but it's not long before they're sowing seeds and taking cuttings and growing exotic South American climbers, lilies from Africa and orchids from the Far East.

We discovered another interesting fact, too. The British have often been accused of being a race of gardeners and, goodness, that's true. Deep down inside each one of us is a love of the soil and a primeval desire to grow things. That desire is there whether we have a garden or not. We spoke to flat-dwellers in London who had never owned a garden, to students in lodgings, even to sixteen-year-old punk rockers with brilliant spikes of orange hair. Each and every one of them had some sort of plant on their windowsill.

So what we have set out to do in both the TV series and this book is to try to breed success.

Certainly we attack the basic problems, especially for

those folk who need help to keep their plants alive. However, there's considerably more excitement in house-plants than just buying a plant from the shop and keeping it alive. If we know anything, you will be wanting to take cuttings, to raise something a bit unusual from seed, and even to produce fruiting plants from those pips brought back from your holiday in southern Spain.

So this is a *doing* book. We deliberately avoided the standard coffee-table glossy that assumes you furnish your mansion from Heal's or Habitat and that the butler will polish the rubber plant. We'll help you raise plants for next to nothing, we'll help you make them flower their little socks off, we'll advise on which to buy and which to leave alone, we'll suggest the best places and conditions for them to thrive and, above all, we'll make darned sure you keep them alive.

Geoff Hamilton
Barnsdale, 1985

NEW PLANTS

Success or failure with houseplants starts even before you walk into the shop to buy one. The very first essential is to decide exactly what kind of plant will survive and flourish in the particular conditions you expect it to adapt to.

It's not a bit of good buying a cyclamen for the centrally heated sitting room and even worse to expect a gloxinia to put up with the unheated spare bedroom.

Think about light, too, before you buy, choosing shade lovers for that dark spot behind the television set and sun worshippers for the bright, south-facing windowsill.

Humidity must also be taken into account. If it's impossible to provide a humid atmosphere, it really isn't worth buying plants such as bromeliads that soak up moisture like little sponges.

Finally, think about your own expertise. If you're unused to growing houseplants, avoid the temptation to be too ambitious. It's much better to succeed first time with a primrose than to fail in the first week with an orchid. That could put you off houseplants for life.

Having decided on the type of plant, think carefully about where you buy it. Bear in mind that plants are raised in perfect conditions in the warmth of a greenhouse. So, if you see a tender plant for sale on an outside market stall in January, hurry quickly by with your eyes averted. In the winter and spring, only hardy plants should be bought from market stalls or shops where the plants are relegated to a draughty spot on the pavement.

Ideally, buy direct from the grower but if that's impossible go to a garden centre where the plants are well looked after or to a heated florist's shop. The large supermarkets now stock a wide range of good houseplants at reasonable prices, and most branches have the expertise and the facilities to look after them.

Finally, look at the plant itself. Reject immediately anything that shows signs of pest or disease attack or that looks wilted or starved or any whose leaves are brown at the edges. Any of these signs show that the plant hasn't been looked after so there may be other, less obvious faults. If you're buying a flowering plant, look for one that's in tight bud so that you'll get plenty of flowering time out of it later. What you are looking for is a plant in the peak of condition because it's going to need all the resilience it can muster.

Having selected a perfect specimen from ideal conditions, you owe it to the plant to coddle it a little on its way home. It will suffer in the winter, even passing from the shop to the car parked right outside. In the nursery, great pains are taken to avoid chill. If plants need to be transferred from one heated house to another, they are put in a 'coffin'. (This is an entirely enclosed and draught-proof box that can be brought right into the greenhouse for loading up.) We should take the same care. When you go on a buying expedition, take a large polythene bag with you that's big enough completely to enclose the plant. Put it in the bottom and tie the top and your plant will have the very best chance of surviving the journey without harm.

Checklist before buying houseplants

- Choose a plant that will enjoy the conditions available;

- Buy from a reputable source where the plants are well looked after;

- Check for signs of pests, disease or deficiency;

- Buy flowering plants in tight bud with plenty more buds to come;

- Take care getting the plant home, especially in the winter.

New plants from seed

This is one of the cheapest ways to raise new houseplants, but it's something that needs care and patience and a fair bit of space. There are many flowering pot plants that are really very simple to grow to maturity in the house, while others, especially foliage plants, can be quite difficult.

If you have a greenhouse or conservatory, it's naturally much easier, but even if you haven't it's certainly not impossible. However, you'll definitely need our home-made light box (page 34). Most seeds require a fairly high temperature to germinate so you'll also need a propagator or the airing cupboard to get them started.

Sow seeds in small pots in special seed compost, which must be thoroughly moistened before you start. Large seeds can be 'space sown', setting them singly in well-spaced stations to avoid early transplanting. Small seeds can be broadcast very thinly over the surface by making use of the special seed-sowing channel provided in every hand especially for the job. Place the seed in your palm and clench it slightly. You'll notice that a channel appears below the last three fingers and the seeds will trickle down this evenly. Simply tap your hand with the index finger of the other one while moving it systematically over the compost.

Begonia semperflorens

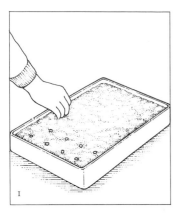

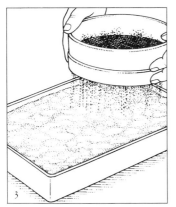

1 'Space sow' large seeds, setting each one well apart

2 Small seeds can be broadcast through your hand

3 Use a fine garden sieve to cover the seeds evenly

If the seed is very, very fine – like that of begonias – it can be mixed with silver sand before sowing to ensure a really even spread.

After sowing, all but the finest seed needs covering. The aim should be to cover to a depth equal to the size of the seed. Therefore tiny seeds, such as begonia, should not be covered at all, while larger ones, such as *Solanum*, should be. A fine garden sieve will help cover the seed evenly.

The required temperature for germination varies considerably, but there is quite a wide margin of error, so don't be put off. I have found that for most seed the shelf immediately above the tank of the airing cupboard is a bit too hot. I use the one above that for almost everything and it works well. Of course, if you have a heated propagator, so much the better.

Before putting the pots in the airing cupboard, pop them into a polythene bag and tie the top with a wire twist. This will help maintain the required humidity and will prevent dirtying the clean linen. In a propagator, the pots or even the whole propagator will have to be covered with opaque polythene to exclude the light until the first seedlings show through. This is not, of course, necessary in the airing cupboard.

It's essential to keep an eye on the seeds every day. I have germinated geraniums in one day in the airing cupboard and, after they come through, they grow very fast indeed. If you forget and leave them for even a day after they appear, they'll become long and straggly and will never make a decent plant.

Just as soon as the first seedlings appear, put them on a sunny windowsill in the light box (see page 34). Be prepared to cover the young seedlings with newspaper if the sun is hot and water them regularly from now on.

Once the seedlings are large enough to handle by the leaves, they can be transferred to their own individual pots. They should never be handled by their delicate stems, so make sure that there is enough of a leaf to grasp. Transfer them first into small pots, using potting compost. If the pot is too large, the compost around the roots of the young seedling will become a wet, cold, soggy mass and young roots won't like that one bit. When the roots start to emerge from the bottom of the pot, the plant can be transferred to a bigger one.

Some easy plants to raise from seed

Flowering
*Abutilon, Begonia, Browallia, Cactus, Calceolaria,
Celosia, Cineraria, Coleus, Cyclamen, Exacum, Freesia,
Geranium, Hypoestes, Impatiens, Primula, Schizanthus,
Solanum, Streptocarpus* and *Vinca.*

Foliage
Aralia, Asparagus, Cyperus, Mimosa and *Schefflera.*

4

Layering

Certainly one of the easiest of all methods of propagation
is by layering. Indeed, some plants all but do it for you.
Those such as the spider plant (*Chlorophytum comosum*) and
the mother of thousands (*Saxifraga stolonifera*) produce
plantlets on the end of long stems. Simply pin the plantlets
into a pot of moist compost and sever from the parent
once well rooted. In fact, so easily do these plants root that
the plantlets can be severed first and then pinned down
and 90 per cent will root.

Other trailing plants such as ivies and the grape ivy
(*Rhoicissus capensis*) do not produce plantlets but can still
be encouraged to root. Place a stem on top of a pot of
moist compost and pin it down with a hairpin or a bent
paperclip, so that a leaf joint is held just below the surface.
Eventually it will start to push up new leaves and stems
from the leaf joint – an indication that it has rooted and is
growing away. It can then be severed from the parent
plant and grown on.

Other plants can be propagated in the same way, but
they are not so accommodating as to bend down to the soil
for you. The rubber plant (*Ficus robusta*) is often increased
by layers but, because it makes a stiff, upright stem the
technique differs in one respect: it's necessary to take the
compost to the layer rather than the other way around. It's
an especially useful method of shortening the height of a
plant which has outgrown the living room and threatens
to break through the ceiling.

Start by making an upward cut into the stem about a
third of the way in. You'll find that, with the rubber plant,
a stream of white latex will start to ooze out. It looks

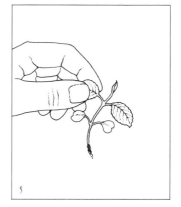

5

4 Protect the young seedlings in
the light box from the hot sun
with newspaper

5 Grasp the seedlings by a
leaf – never the delicate stem –
to transfer to individual pots

6 A mother of thousands (*Saxifraga stolonifera*) plant is layered by pinning the plantlet into a pot of moist compost

7 Layer a trailing grape ivy by pinning the stem on either side of a leaf joint

Browallia 'Blue Troll'

drastic but it's no problem. Dust the cut with a little hormone rooting powder and then pack some damp sphagnum moss into the cut to keep it just open. (You can buy this from the florist.) Then pack a little more moist peat around the stem and hold it in place with polythene, held onto the stem top and bottom with sticky tape.

It may take some time for the layer to root, so take a look at it from time to time and moisten the moss if necessary. Once you do see roots coming through, the polythene can be removed and the new plant cut off below where it has rooted. Pot it up individually without disturbing the moss. The old plant can be grown on though it will probably grow two stems above the cut.

Cuttings

The most common method of producing new plants is to take a piece of stem or a leaf and to encourage it to produce roots and, eventually, a new plant. To do this sometimes requires artificial conditions and a certain amount of equipment. Heat is often essential and here the airing cupboard won't do because the plants will need light. A heated propagator is the only answer. However, there are also several plants that root easily with the most primitive of equipment and no extra heat.

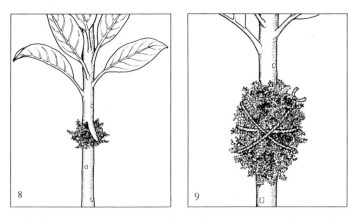

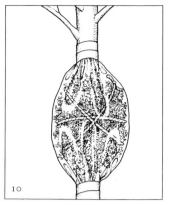

Softwood cuttings are taken from the tips of growing stems. Generally the best time to take them is when the plant has recently started into active growth – June is often good. The length of cuttings varies but a good rule is to make them at least three leaf joints long. Cut the

8 Make an upward cut in the stem of the rubber plant

9 Pack more moist peat around the stem.

10 Hold the peat in place with polythene

Left: *Calceolaria*

Above: *Cissus rhombifolia* 'Ellen Danica'

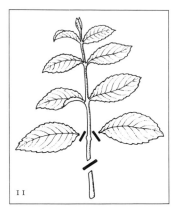

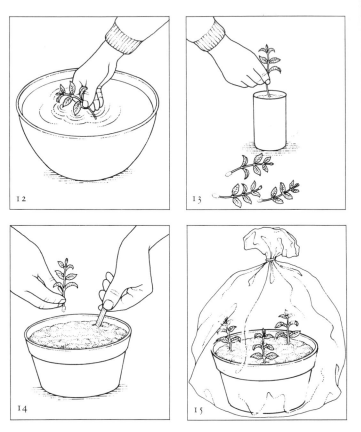

11 A softwood cutting is taken from a growing stem, four leaf joints below the tip

12 Dip the whole cutting in a solution of Benlate

13 Dip the end of the cutting into hormone rooting powder

14 Use a pencil to make a small hole in the compost as you put the cutting in it

15 Make sure the sides of the polythene bag do not touch the cuttings

shoot off the plant, leaving four leaf joints, and then trim just below a leaf, using a very sharp knife or a razor blade.

Not all cuttings require the use of hormone rooting powder and, in fact, some such as geraniums are actually discouraged from rooting if you do use it. But they should all be dipped into a solution of fungicide before setting them in the compost. Make up a solution of Benlate, according to the maker's instructions, and dip the whole cutting into it. Then, if recommended, dip the end of the cutting into hormone rooting powder and shake off the excess by gently tapping it on the side of the container.

Put the cuttings into small pots of seed compost or a mixture of half peat and half perlite. No fertiliser is necessary. When you put them into the compost, make a small hole first, perhaps with a pencil, then put in the cuttings and gently firm them. If you simply push them in, you may remove the rooting powder.

If the cuttings need heat, place the pot in the propagator and cover it with the plastic lid. Alternatively, put the pot into a plastic bag and blow it up like a balloon to keep the cuttings from touching the sides. Tie the top and put it above a source of heat such as the radiator – but not so close as to cook it. Naturally this site won't be as satisfactory if the radiator is set to go off at night – and, alas, most are.

As the cuttings are still making food through their leaves while they're rooting, they will need sunshine. On the other hand, too much sunshine will make them lose water quickly and they'll wilt. So, try to strike the happy medium by putting the pots in a light place but out of direct sunshine. If the propagator is in the greenhouse or conservatory, it may be necessary to cover it with a piece of net shading material.

Some cuttings are very fast to root and will need no further watering before they are taken out and potted up. Others take a long time and should be checked frequently. If any show signs of rotting, remove them immediately. If the compost begins to dry out, water it again using the Benlate solution.

Some plants, such as *Dracaena, Dieffenbachia* and even geraniums, can be increased by stem sections. The advantage is that the parent plant will produce many more cuttings this way.

Simply cut off a stem and cut it into sections between the leaf joints. Lay the sections on moist compost in a deep box and cover with plastic sheeting. When the sections begin to sprout small leaves, they will have rooted and they must then be 'weaned'. It would be too much of a shock to remove the plastic sheeting immediately, so cut a slit in it the first day, increasing the opening gradually over about a fortnight until the sheet is removed entirely.

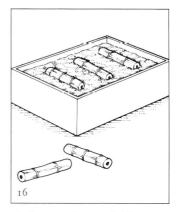

16 Stem sections are laid on moist compost in a deep box to root

Leaf cuttings

A very few plants will make new plants from their leaves. The most popular for this method is the African violet, which will root very easily. However, not all the leaves will do, so old leaves and very young leaves should be ignored. Look towards the middle of the plant and take leaves that are neither the youngest nor the oldest. Cut them off carefully, trying to avoid leaving a snag, which might rot and spoil the parent plant. It's important

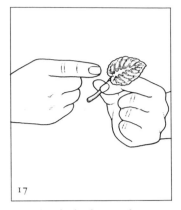

17 Trim the leaf stem of an African violet by tapping with your index finger to make a clean break

to cut the leaf stem very cleanly without bruising the tender tissue. The best way to do this is to hold the leaf gently in one hand and to tap the leaf stem sharply with the index finger of the other. It should snap off as clean as a whistle.

There are two ways to root the leaves – either in water or in compost. The snag with the water method, though very fast and successful, is that the roots are of a different type to those it makes in compost. So, when the plant is transferred to compost, it has more or less to start again and this can result in losses. The answer is to transfer water-rooted cuttings when the roots are only just visible.

To root them in water, take a jam jar full of water and cover the top with kitchen foil. Make a couple of holes in the top and poke the leaf stems through so that they hang in the water. Put them in a semi-shaded spot and keep a close eye for those young roots.

The commercial growers never mess about with nonsense like that. They root them directly in a seed compost or the 50:50 peat and perlite mix.

Begonia rex – the superb foliage begonia – can be rooted in the same way or, if you want several plants, the leaf can be pinned down onto the surface of the compost after making a series of small cuts in the veins on the underside of the leaf. This plant will need a fair bit of heat – about 21 °C (70 °F), so there's little point in propagating in this way unless you have a propagator.

Saintpaulia 'Laura'
(African violet)

Begonia rex 'Bettina Rothschild'

Cacti and succulents root quite readily from cuttings. The desert types, such as *Opuntia*, that make branched stems are perhaps the easiest. Simply remove an 'ear' but be careful, because they'll often take their revenge by filling your fingers with spines. Leave the ear to dry out in the sun for a few days and then push it into the seed compost. Ideally put it on a shelf over a radiator where it will be heated to about 21 °C (70 °F). Much the same technique can be used for *Epiphyllums* and *Zygocactus*.

Root division

Plants that produce stems from below compost level can often be divided, although it's best not to be too ambitious. Even if there are dozens of stems rising from the base of the plant, don't try to make too many new plants from the one – simply divide the plant into two.

Plants such as the asparagus fern can be gently prised apart by hand but others with tough, fleshy roots, like mother-in-law's tongue, will have to be cut through. The bread knife is an ideal tool for this job.

18 Root the leaf stems by suspending them in water

19 The leaf cuttings will also root directly in a seed compost

20 Pin a begonia leaf cutting onto the surface of the compost

21 Taking a cactus stem cutting by removing an 'ear'

22 A bread knife is the ideal tool to prise apart the tough, fleshy roots of mother-in-law's tongue

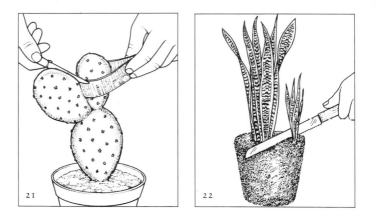

After repotting, give the new plants a good watering and put them in a shady spot. Don't rewater until the compost dries right out, so as to encourage the plant to put out new young roots in search of water.

Plants such as *Achimenes* and some orchids grow from rhizomes – fleshy storage organs that look like thick roots. In the spring, when they are just starting into new growth, they can be divided to produce several new plants.

Knock the plant out of the pot and gently tease the individual rhizomes from the compost. You'll be able to see new growth buds on each section of the rhizome and each one of these will make a new plant. If you have the patience and want that many plants, cut the rhizome between each joint. But to make good-sized new plants in as short a time as possible, it's best to leave several buds on each section. They can be rooted by putting them in a seed tray or a largish pot of compost. Put a shallow layer of silver sand on top of the compost and gently work the sections into it. Ideally, they should have a little gentle heat underneath, so either set them in a propagator in a slightly shaded spot or over the radiator. Once they've rooted, they should be potted on into straight potting compost at the same level the parent plant was before it was removed.

Plants like begonias, that grow from tubers, can also be divided. In fact, after a few years begonia tubers will become enormous and too unwieldy for a pot, so division becomes necessary.

In about February, put the tubers on a bed of compost

in a seed tray and put it in a slightly heated propagator or over the radiator. After a week or two, you'll be able to see new growths appearing and this will give a clue as to where to cut. Each section should have one good growth – but preferably three or four – on it. After cutting, rub a little fungicide powder into the wound – either sulphur or Benlate, whichever you've got – just to be on the safe side. Then pot up each piece individually in potting compost so that the top half of the tuber is above the compost level.

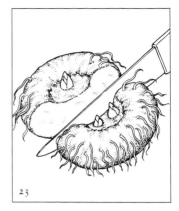

Offsets
Several plants produce offsets at their base. These are really small plants which may already be rooted. Those that have can simply be removed and repotted, taking care to break as little root as possible. If the offsets don't have any roots, either gently pull or cut them from the parent and press them into a pot or tray of compost topped with a shallow layer of silver sand. Again, a little heat at the bottom will help.

New plants from bulbs, corms and tubers
Generally, this is a pretty easy and almost certain way to produce flowering plants for the house. There are two main times for planting: in the spring and early summer for those that flower in summer and autumn; and in the late summer and autumn for the spring-flowering subjects. These require rather a different technique.

23 Divide begonia tubers when you see the new growths appear

24 Offsets should be carefully removed from the base of the parent plant for repotting

Bulbs planted in the spring are generally set either on top of the compost or with their 'noses' just poking out. They can simply be put on the windowsill and allowed to develop. With some of them, it's a bit difficult to see which way up they should be planted. Gloxinias and sometimes begonias are perhaps the hardest to decide about. If you can't make up your mind, put them in a polythene bag with a little moist peat. Leave the bag in a warm place and, in a few days, the corms or tubers will begin to sprout. These sprouts will be shoots which must, of course, go upwards.

With spring-flowering bulbs, such as hyacinths and daffodils, it's essential to allow a good root to develop before the top growth starts. To do this, they need a cool, dark spot. They are potted in August if the bulbs have been especially prepared for Christmas flowering or in September for spring flowering, using potting compost if

Above: Hyacinth 'Anne Marie'

Right: Daffodil 'Bartley'

they are grown in well-drained pots, or special bulb fibre if they are set in bowls with no drainage holes.

They should then be plunged under a good deep layer of peat out of doors. If that's impossible, put them in a dark cupboard, but make sure it's in the coolest part of the house, since it's important not to encourage the top growth to develop.

Have a look at the pots from time to time and, when the growths are 2–3 in. (5–7.5 cm.) high, bring them into a cool, shaded room. Later they can be introduced to more heat and light ready for flowering.

New plants from pips

Several of the fruits we eat will yield seeds that will eventually grow into attractive and often interesting house-plants. It may even be possible to get some of them to bear fruit, eventually.

Avocados

These are started off in water. Remove the stone and suspend it in a jam jar of water by sticking a couple of hairpins or three matchsticks in the sides and resting these on the rim of the jar. Put the jar in the airing cupboard – which by now should be so full of plants there'll be no room for clothes. Ideally keep it at a temperature of about 21°C (70°F). Eventually a root should emerge, but it's best still to keep it in the airing cupboard until the shoot starts to grow. Then it must be removed immediately.

Allow the root to develop well and then pot up into soilless compost. Some pruning of the top is desirable to form a well-branched plant and feeding should start about six weeks after potting.

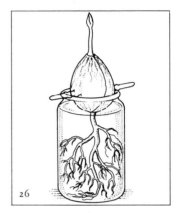

25 Bulbs should preferably be left out of doors under a good deep covering of peat

26 Suspend an avocado stone over a jam jar of water and put in the airing cupboard to root

Peanuts

Fascinating plants these, by any standards, in that they physically bend down and sow their own seeds – that's if you can get them to the seeding stage, which is not easy. They are easy to germinate and to grow on though, so they're a great deal of fun to grow. Make sure you get unroasted nuts, preferably in their shells.

Peanuts are best sown in April and you can either crack the shell and put the nuts in separately or sow the whole lot with the shells on. If you do the latter, there's a great upheaval of compost when they germinate and push sky-wards with the pod fixed to the growing point.

Sow three or four nuts in the centre of a large pot – about 6–7in. (15–17.5cm.) diameter is ideal – and put them in the airing cupboard or propagator at about 21°C (70°F). After germination grow them on in a light, sunny position and don't feed them at all.

Dates

These have very hard shells and are best put into moist peat in a polythene bag in the airing cupboard. Keep looking at them and remove any that show signs of sprouting. They can be potted immediately, taking great care not to damage the sprouted root. Grow them on in a warm, light place.

Citrus fruits

Oranges and lemons make good houseplants with attractive foliage, and there is always the not-so-remote chance of getting them to fruit. The best time to sow the seeds is in the spring so they can benefit from the summer's light in order to make a reasonable plant before winter.

Ideally, sow them no more than ½in. (13mm.) deep, individually in small pots of soilless compost, and put them on a high shelf in the airing cupboard or in the propagator. They need a temperature of about 15–18°C (60–65°F).

As soon as shoots show through, bring them into full light and, after about six weeks, begin to feed. Repot them when the roots fill the pot.

New plants from the garden

Every house has its problem places for houseplants, the most common being those parts that are cold or draughty. The hallway is often bad and an enclosed porch or even an unheated conservatory can be difficult, especially in the

27 Date stones will sprout if you put them in a polythene bag of moist compost

28 Orange and lemon seeds sown singly in small pots will make attractive houseplants. Begin to feed them after six weeks

winter and spring. It's not a bit of good trying to grow some delicate prima donna of the jungle there, but these places are ideal for hardy plants from the garden.

The spring-flowering plants are most valuable because they'll grow where nothing else will. Indeed, though they will hang on to life for a while in a centrally heated living room, they'll be much happier where it's cold.

Easy plants to grow as houseplants
From pips
Avocados, dates, grapefruit, lemons, oranges, peanuts and tangerines.

Hardy plants
Azalea, Dicentra, Erica, Helleborus, Jasminum and *Primula.*

Half-hardy/bedding plants
Begonia, Calceolaria, Campanula, Fuchsia, geraniums, *Impatiens, Nemesia, Nicotiana* (dwarf) and *Salvia.*

The sort of plants to grow are things like spring-flowering primulas, Christmas rose (*Helleborus niger*), *Dicentra spectabilis* and *Erica carnea* varieties. Lift them about October time and shake off as much of the garden soil as possible without damaging the roots. Then pot them into $3\frac{1}{2}$ or 4in. (9 or 10cm.) pots and put them in a cool spot, ideally out of direct sunlight.

They will flower earlier than their counterparts still in the garden and, without the rigours of the weather to contend with, they'll produce more flowers of a much better quality. After flowering, they are best returned to the garden where they'll be much happier. If you don't have a garden, put the pots outside for the spring and summer and water and feed them. They should do quite well enough to be brought in for another flowering the following year.

At the other end of the season, it's worthwhile lifting a few summer-flowering plants that would otherwise be caught by the frost. Fibrous-rooted begonias and *Impatiens* are ideal. They can be cut back a little, removing all the dead leaves and flowers, and be potted up into small pots. Inside a cool room, they'll flower well into the new year.

Above: *Fuchsia magellanica gracilis*
Right: *Campanula isophylla*

One of the cheapest ways to fill your rooms with colour during the summer is with half-hardy bedding plants, which you can buy in the garden centre. These are really intended for bedding out in the garden. Potted up, many of them make superb houseplants which can be kept in flower all summer long, provided they are kept reasonably cool.

Perennials such as fuchsias and geraniums can be kept year after year and, indeed, I've seen fuchsias in particular that just never stop flowering, even in the winter.

The annuals, such as petunias, salvias and the superb new *Campanula isophylla* 'Kristal' varieties, make really excellent pot plants that will flower their hearts out. They can all be raised quite easily from seed on the windowsill or be bought as plants in the garden centre. Keep them as cool as possible yet in a sunny spot and feed them once a fortnight during the summer.

If perhaps you have a porch or a balcony that remains cold, considerable interest and colour can be obtained from alpine plants. Hardly houseplants these, but worth a mention for otherwise difficult cold places. However, they must be kept as cold as possible, so don't even attempt them for long periods in the centrally heated living room. Much better, grow them to flowering either in pots outside or in an unheated and well-ventilated greenhouse, and bring them in for just a day or two when they're at their best.

Alpines need a very well-drained compost so mix about equal parts of John Innes potting compost with sharp, coarse grit and put plenty of drainage in the bottom of the pot. During the winter they should be kept almost dry and will need only sparing watering during the summer. They require very little food so only add fertiliser to the water if they appear to be growing badly.

Petunia 'Satellite'

EQUIPMENT

As you would expect, the growing interest in houseplants
has spawned a new industry – equipment the good houseplant grower can't do without. The garden centres are full
of gadgets from miniature forks and trowels to computers
that will tell you everything you want to know about your
plant from when it needs water to whether or not it's lonely
or depressed. As you would also expect, most of them are
unnecessary. Why buy a miniature stainless steel fork when
a wooden plant label will do? With a little prudence, houseplant care needn't cost much. Naturally, though, some
equipment will be necessary, some of which must be
bought and some you can make.

Pots

There are two types of flower pots – plastic and clay. Both
have advantages and disadvantages.

There's no doubt that clay looks better than plastic
though you'll have to pay for that advantage because they
are considerably more expensive. However, bear in mind
that the wide range of decorative plant-pot covers available makes it unnecessary to see the pot.

Clay pots are also heavier than plastic and this can be a
considerable advantage. Large leafy houseplants can become
very unstable, especially if they are potted into soilless
compost. Once they get top heavy they fall over, especially
when the compost dries out. Though this may be a convenient indication that the compost needs watering, it's a
pretty drastic reminder! A clay pot, especially combined
with a heavier, soil-based compost, will solve the problem.

The main difference between clay and plastic is the
porosity of clay. Air and water will pass through the wall
of a clay pot, and this will certainly not occur with plastic.
Thus clay pots are ideal for those plants, such as the
popular mother-in-law's tongue, that like to be kept on
the dry side.

That is not to say that you can't grow moisture lovers in
clay pots or those that like it dry in plastic. However, you
must be aware that the compost in clay pots will always
dry out more quickly. For this reason, I like to use soil-
based composts in clay pots and soilless in plastic.

Composts

Plants growing in pots are in an entirely artificial environment, so they need careful treatment. However fertile you may feel your garden soil to be, it will *never* do for pot-grown plants. The soil will pack down to become mud when watered and concrete when it dries out. No plant will be happy in that, so a special compost is vital.

If you've ever bought a houseplant, it will almost certainly have been potted into a peat compost. Growers long ago turned over almost completely to peat, when good fibrous topsoil became almost impossible to come by and, on the whole, their reliance on it is justified. Certainly the so-called John Innes, soil-based composts available today are so variable that you risk buying poor quality every time.

However, there are some plants that will much prefer a soil-based compost because of its better drainage and indeed some, such as cacti, like it even more freely drained. The only advice it's possible to give when buying John Innes is to take it back if you're not satisfied. Indeed I always cut the bag open in the shop and risk an argument!

If you're really keen, you can mix your own composts to the John Innes formula, but it's not a job I would recommend. In small quantities, it's extremely difficult to mix in the necessary chemicals so that they are perfectly evenly distributed and this could have disastrous results. It's better to rely on the commercially mixed products.

There is no real standard for peat-based composts and different manufacturers have different recipes of their own. You pays your money and you takes your choice. However, the research done for commercial growers indicates that a mix of 75 per cent sphagnum peat and 25 per cent perlite makes an ideal general-purpose compost. There are manufacturers that make up composts to this formula plus the necessary lime and fertilisers. You can recognise those containing perlite by the white specks that look something like expanded polystyrene.

If you decide to mix your own, which I must say is as fraught with problems as the home-mixed soil-based compost is, be careful to choose the right grades of peat and of perlite.

There are two types of peat – sedge peat and sphagnum moss peat. The sedge is almost black and looks so much more fertile than the moss peat that most gardeners would prefer it. Alas, it isn't more fertile and it's quite unsuitable for composts.

Because it's older, sedge peat is less open than moss peat, so when it's watered it compacts to form an airless mass. To make matters worse, the rate of compaction seems to be quite unpredictable, so you could finish up with a dozen pots of plants all the same and all potted at the same time but all requiring different amounts of water. In short, never use it for potting.

The general rule is that the lighter the peat is in colour, and the coarser it appears to be, the better – just the reverse of what you would think. Apparently commercial growers have been known to sell their grandmothers to get their hands on what is called 'white peat' – a very light coloured one from Finland, which is the very cream. So far, it isn't available to home gardeners so use either Irish or British moss peat.

The quality of perlite also varies greatly and it's important to get the right one. This is a volcanic rock, expanded by heat to form a granular, porous material ideal for aerating composts and improving drainage. It's also excellent for insulation so it's used widely in the building industry and is on sale to do-it-yourself enthusiasts for this purpose. However, the building grade is not suitable for composts: it is ungraded, so it contains a high percentage of very small particles and dust. These will clog the air spaces between the peat granules and so do the reverse of the function it's intended for. So buy your perlite from the garden centre rather than the ironmonger or builders' merchant and make sure the bag is marked 'Horticultural Perlite'.

Again, you'll need about 1oz (28gm) of ground chalk or garden lime per 2gal. (9.1 litre) bucketful of peat.

There are two ways of providing the necessary plant food. I've tried both over a long period and many different plants and have found both methods completely successful.

The first is to use the John Innes base fertiliser as per the instructions on the pack. It should be mixed in as large a quantity as possible to try to ensure an even distribution and for this reason is really only feasible if you're intending to pot a large number of plants.

The alternative method is to add no fertiliser at all but to feed with a liquid fertiliser right from the start. The only reservation here is that if the plants are young, it's prudent to start with a dilute solution. In fact I start off with a half-strength feed until the young plants have established a good root system.

Special composts

A few classes of houseplant demand special treatment and it's well worthwhile starting off with the correct compost. For all these special cases, composts can be bought ready mixed, but it's not difficult to mix your own since most are only a case of adding to an existing mix.

Cacti, succulents and alpines all require very free drainage. They are best grown in John Innes compost plus coarse grit. And the grit must be really coarse. Sand, even sharp sand, is not nearly coarse enough, and you should never, never dream of using builders' sand – the fine orange stuff – which is worse than useless. You can buy horticultural coarse grit in a garden centre and you should settle for nothing less. If you add one part of grit to two parts of John Innes No. 1 potting compost, you'll have an ideal mix for cacti and succulents. For alpines you can go overboard and use equal parts of grit and John Innes No. 1, because alpines like nothing better than really sharp drainage. No extra lime or fertiliser is needed.

Left: *Rhododendron* 'Leopold Astrid'

Above: *Erica carnea* 'Myretoun Ruby'

Below: Christmas cactus

Bromeliads, azaleas, heathers and rhododendrons must have an acid compost. They can be potted in pure peat and fed with liquid fertiliser right from the start, or you can buy a special, peat-based 'ericaceous compost', which has the right degree of acidity plus the necessary fertiliser.

Orchids and carnivorous plants also need special composts. They used to be grown in a stuff called 'osmunda fibre', and this is still often recommended. I must say that I haven't seen any for sale for about twenty years! Fortunately there is an alternative and all the ingredients are available.

You'll need coarse pine bark, a white granular substance used on greenhouse stagings called Perlag and our old friend perlite, plus a small amount of charcoal. All are available at good garden centres. Mix three parts of bark with one each of Perlag and perlite plus a sprinkling of charcoal chippings – about a handful to a bucketful of compost will do but the amount is not critical. No fertiliser or lime is necessary.

I have also suggested earlier in the book that you may want to lift a few plants from the garden to use in the house. Let me just say again that, because plants are happy in garden soil outside, it doesn't mean that they'll like it in a pot. So shake off what soil you can and pot them in a container large enough to hold a large quantity of proper potting compost.

Seed and cuttings composts

If you intend to raise your own plants from seeds or cuttings, you'll need a special compost for them. Certainly the best bet there is to buy a proprietary peat-based compost specially prepared for the job.

Compost additives

A new development in the commercial field has now become available to amateurs. Some growers are now adding a granular polymer to composts to assist with watering problems. The polymer has the capacity of holding about one hundred times its own volume of water, making water available to the plant as and when it's needed.

However, as you would imagine, for those folk who tend to coddle their plants with a little drop of water each day, this extra water-holding capacity could spell disaster. In my view, polymers should not be used in the compost mix because they would only make the already widespread habit of overwatering worse.

However, it's also possible to buy the material in a small sachet that can be put in the bottom of the pot. It looks just like a tea-bag and will sit at the bottom of the pot allowing water in and out again as the plant requires it. My own trials have shown that this reduces the necessity for watering quite considerably but, since the extra reservoir is near the bottom of the pot, excess water drains away in the normal way.

Propagators

It you intend to raise your own plants from seeds or cuttings, a propagator is invaluable. The aim with all propagation is to keep the temperature even – a very difficult feat in the house, where central heating could raise the temperature during the day only to allow it to plummet at night.

Even enclosing plants in an unheated glass or plastic case will help to even out the temperature, but the ideal is a thermostatically controlled propagator. These are electrically heated and can be set to maintain continually any temperature that is likely to be required. You can even buy a long, slim propagator made espccially to fit on the windowsill. Propagators that include thermostatic controls are rather expensive. A cheaper alternative is the uncontrolled propagator. This docs not include a thermostat though it is electrically heated. In my view, it is generally adequate for all but the most difficult plants and it costs a fraction of the price of the more sophisticated type.

An unheated propagator is fine for use during the summer but, unless you can put it over a regular heat source both day and night, it has limited use for germination during the winter. However, most of us have an airing cupboard which maintains a pretty constant heat day and night. That heat can be utilised to germinate seeds because most do not, of course, need light. Once germinated, they require a lower temperature regime, so the unheated propagator could be used for all but the most difficult subjects.

Light boxes

Seedlings are pretty easy to germinate in the propagator or the airing cupboard. Then, all they need is heat and water,

29 A thermostatically controlled heated propagator is the ideal – but they are expensive

30 An unheated propagator can be used in summer

29

30

but, once germinated, they are hungry for light – and that's one of the greatest problems of raising seedlings on the windowsill.

However sunny your window may seem, in the winter and early spring there won't really be enough light for those vigorous young seedlings so eager to grow away. Even a greenhouse with double the amount of light needs to be kept scrupulously clean to harvest all the light available. Without light, seedlings become long, leggy and weak. They make less attractive houseplants and are prone to disease. What is needed is to trap every available bit of light – and you can do it for just a few pence.

Start with a deep wooden orange or apple box and knock out one side, leaving only the very bottom slat. Then tack a thin strip of wood across the top. Ideally, the inside of the box should be lined with polystyrene to retain all the heat possible. Ceiling tiles are relatively cheap and ideal for the job. Then line the inside walls and the bottom with kitchen foil. This reflective surface will trap all the sunlight there is and throw it back onto the plants.

To keep the seedlings warm at night, tack a small sheet of polythene on the back of the box and fix a strip of wood to the front edge. This will act as a weight to hold the sheet down when it's put over the top of the box.

Site the light box in the sunniest window during the day but bring it in nearer the middle of the room at night. Never draw the curtains between the box and the room. It's at night, too, that the polythene should be drawn over the box to retain all the heat possible. Bear in mind that even a sheet of clear polythene can prevent a considerable amount of light entering the box, so remove it again as early as possible in the day. Just one word of warning. You may find that on sunny days, even in winter, the sun is hot enough to shrivel small seedlings, so be prepared to shade with a few sheets of newspaper.

Thermometers

Maintaining the correct temperature for houseplants is critical. Different types need different temperatures and will not do well if they're too hot or too cold. It's important therefore to know the average temperature but much more important to know the *extremes* of hot and cold your plants have to endure. That's what will determine success or failure. Since you won't be sitting up with your plants

31 Tack a sheet of polythene to the back of the light box to protect the seedlings at night

32 A maximum/minimum thermometer

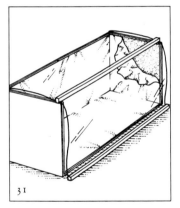

31

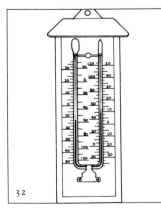

32

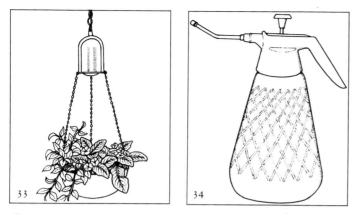

33 You need a special bulb to provide artificial light – fix it about 3ft. (90cm.) above the plants

34 A hand sprayer is an essential piece of equipment

all night or indeed keeping them company all day, you need a thermometer that will record the extremes. A maximum/minimum thermometer will do just that. Two mercury-filled tubes push up a small float that will remain at both the highest and the lowest points, telling you at any time the temperature extremes reached since you last set it. They are not expensive and one could make all the difference.

Lighting

However dark the recesses of your room, you can grow plants there – but you may need the help of artificial lighting. Normal electric lights are useless for growing plants. They produce far more heat than they do light and, if you position them where they'll provide sufficient light, the heat generated will burn your plants to a frazzle.

Fluorescent tubes are better, but, ideally, use a special bulb. These use special filaments and filling that provide a light that is almost identical to sunlight. They are available as tubes or ordinary bulbs with either a screw or bayonet fitting. One bulb will light an area some 5ft (150cm.) in diameter and should be fixed about 3ft (90cm.) above the plants. Unless you're a very competent electrician, it's best to employ a contractor to fix the unit for you.

Sprayers

A small hand sprayer is an essential piece of equipment – indeed I always keep two. What is more, I have made sure they are pretty posh-looking sprayers, too. That way, I leave at least one around in the living room where I can see it and it's instantly available.

Most plants require much more humidity than we can give them in the living room, so they'll relish a cool spray with clear water each and every time you can remember. If you leave the sprayer full of water, and in full view, you're much more likely to use it. The other sprayer I use purely for pest and disease control, so I have made sure they are both very clearly marked so there's no chance of getting them mixed up.

Essential equipment and materials

- Several sizes of pots;
- Plastic saucers;
- $\frac{1}{8}$in. (3mm.) gravel;
- Proprietary soilless compost or sphagnum moss peat and perlite;
- John Innes base fertiliser;
- John Innes No. 2 potting compost;
- Soilless seed compost;
- General liquid fertiliser;
- Liquid tomato fertiliser;
- Home-made light box;
- Polythene bags;
- Maximum and minimum thermometer;
- Sprayer;
- Houseplant insecticide and fungicide.

CARE

Many years ago I talked at length to an American lie-detector expert who was convinced that plants had feelings and could more or less think for themselves. He had attached the terminals of his lie detector to the leaves of a plant, which had responded in a quite remarkable way. The most dramatic reaction on the lie detector came when he brought another plant into the room and proceeded to tear it to pieces. When he approached the experimental plant, as if to do the same, the needle on the meter quivered violently as if the plant expected the same treatment.

Whether that proves anything or not I couldn't say, but I have certainly seen houseplants that seem to be growing very well because their owners talk to them. I really do believe that makes a difference and I'll tell you why. The folk who talk to their plants treat them with tender loving care. If they are interested enough in them to chat, then you can bet your life they take the trouble to care for them in the best possible way – and that doesn't always mean coddling them. It's often better to leave a plant waterless and cold than to pamper it like a newborn babe.

What is essential is to find out the sort of conditions each houseplant requires. This is generally related to its environment in the wild. As suggested earlier, try to find these out even before you buy so that you know you can provide each plant with optimum conditions. Mind you, there are in theory so many factors affecting plant growth that you may well feel that there will be nothing at all you can grow. The two biggest problems, for example, are temperature and humidity.

I know of no climate in the world that matches that of a centrally heated house. With temperatures at least 32°C (90°F) during the day and down to about 4°C (40°F) at night, the plants are in a pretty unnatural environment. Add to that the fact that, if you provided them with the humidity they know in the wild, all your carpets would rot and you can see that conditions are far from ideal.

However, don't despair. Plants are very resilient indeed and you can often provide a local environment that is at least tolerable. Set the heat and light as near as you can to the ideal and make sure you never neglect them and you'll grow houseplants that will give you literally years of pleasure – even if you can't think of anything to talk to them about.

Position

There are very few houseplants that like to be in the full glare of the sun. This is particularly evident with young plants whose foliage is tender and liable to scorch. If you grow seedlings on the windowsill especially, always be ready to put a piece of newspaper over them when the sun is at its brightest.

Be careful with windows that face south, south-east or south-west. While many plants will thrive there during the winter, they may have to be moved inside to a slightly less sunny spot in the heat of summer. As soon as you see signs of leaf-scorch, if plants develop brown spots or patches or if the young leaves wilt when the sun is out, suspect a touch of sunstroke and move the plants to a shadier position. As a general rule, plants will suffer less when the light intensity is lower than the optimum rather than when it's higher.

Next in the scale of brightness is the west-facing window. It can be quite hot in the summer evenings just as the sun's setting, but generally it's the safest position for plants that need indirect sunlight.

The east-facing window gets most of its sunshine first thing in the morning and it's quite likely that in the summer the curtains may be drawn then. For plants that like sunshine, it would be a kindness to try to remember to draw the curtains back before you go to bed.

The north-facing window is naturally the darkest of all. Still, it gets some light and will still be the lightest place in the room if it's the only window. Sometimes we simply have to make the best of what there is.

Bear in mind that plants will always try to 'reach' for the light. What actually happens is that those cells that are furthest from the light will grow faster than those on the sunny side. So, with one side of the stem elongating quicker than the other, the plant will get itself into a twist and lean towards the light. It's a good idea to turn foliage plants a little every day to avoid this. Don't do it with flowering plants though, because you'll risk losing the flowers or the flower buds.

35 Plants will reach for the light unless you turn them a little each day

Some flowering plants also react to the number of hours of daylight they receive. There are some that will flower better if they have a long day, and others that need only a few hours. So make sure you look at the care instructions on the label of any plant you are unfamiliar with and put it in exactly the right place.

Bear in mind, too, that plants that have become accustomed to the lower light intensity of a windowsill – even one that gets a lot of sun – may suffer when put outside for the summer rest. Plants like azaleas are especially prone to sun-scorch, so put them in a shady spot. Even those that like plenty of sun should be slowly acclimatised to the brighter conditions by a short spell against a north-facing wall first.

Shade lovers can normally go well inside the room, though it may be wise to move some a little nearer the window in winter. In some houses, there may be places where even plants used to deep shade will have insufficient light, but even here plants can be grown with the aid of artificial lights.

As suggested on page 35, it's essential to use a special bulb or tube to represent natural sunlight almost exactly. The bulbs can be used in an ordinary room light fitting or as a spotlight shining on the plants, or they can be concealed above the plants to very good effect.

Temperature

It goes without saying that you must check on the temperature requirements of a plant *before* buying it, to make sure that it will survive in the position you intend for it. Don't think that, because a plant is hardy enough to put up with low temperatures, it will do much better in higher ones. That simply isn't true. A plant that is used to living at low temperatures in the wild will suffer just as much in heat as would a tropical plant in frost.

But I'm afraid it's not quite as easy as that. When considering the choice of plant for a particular spot, as explained earlier, it's not enough to consider the average temperature. What is important is the extremes. To find out how cold your room becomes at night and how hot during the day, you'll need a maximum/minimum thermometer. You may well be surprised when you discover the variation in temperature.

It is better to keep a plant slightly too cold or slightly

36 Draw the curtain between the plants and the window at night

too hot than to allow the temperature to vary too much. Few plants will be happy if the temperature soars during the day and falls dramatically at night. Indeed not many will tolerate a difference of more than about 6°C (10°F) for long.

Now I agree that, with most modern houses being centrally heated, it's difficult to avoid great temperature variations. I'm certainly not suggesting that you sit shivering during the winter, swathed in half-a-dozen jumpers in order that your plants should not suffer. However, there are ways of reducing the variation a little.

Obviously, the position of the plant in relation to the heat source makes a considerable difference. Bear in mind that the nearer a plant is to the radiator, the greater will be the temperature difference when it cools down at night. It would be far better to put the plant near the middle of the room so that it's cooler during the day.

Exactly the same rule applies to plants near a source of cold. During the winter, it's essential to bring plants away from the windowsill at night and never, never draw the curtains between a plant and the room, leaving it to freeze out there on the chilly windowsill all night.

Finally, one other point to consider is the relationship between the temperature and the available light. In temperate regions, plants grow fastest in the summer. This is because there is a rise in temperature coupled with an increase in light intensity. In the winter both drop and the plant takes a rest. It requires less water and feed and it stops growing completely. Indeed some plants will naturally die right down to the ground. That rest period is essential for the plant and should be reproduced in the house.

If you increase the temperature in the winter, which often happens when the central heating goes on in the autumn, and continue watering and feeding, the plant will suffer. Its shoots will become long and weak as it struggles to find enough light to manufacture food, and it will begin to look tired and unhappy. It needs that rest, so it may be worthwhile moving it to another, cooler position and you should certainly reduce water and food.

Tropical plants, on the other hand, experience little change in temperature or light intensity throughout the year. In the wild, they simply continue to grow, often flowering at any old time, just as the fancy takes them. If you can reproduce those conditions in the house, with artificial light as well as heat, you too could keep them growing. Generally, that is too expensive a proposition, so it's best to treat them as you would their cousins from the temperate regions and give them a rest too.

Humidity

The amount of water vapour in the air has a great effect on plant growth. Plants take up water via their roots, passing it up through the plant tissue and finally again through the leaves. If the air is dry, water is lost through the leaves faster than the roots can replace it, and they will wilt.

Of course, some plants have adapted to hot dry conditions in the wild and are well able to cope with it. Cacti, for example, can live in conditions where the humidity is almost zero and fleshy-leaved succulents need little more. Thin-leaved plants from the tropics, however, are much more demanding. They live in the hot steamy jungles where high rainfall and great heat combine to produce an atmosphere like a Turkish bath. Naturally it would be impossible to create humidity like this in the house – but it is possible to go some way to providing the kind of conditions required.

The first thing is to bear humidity in mind when you buy your plants. Those that require very high temperatures and humidity levels should realistically be confined to the heated greenhouse or conservatory. Between the tropical plants and the cacti, there is a whole range of plants requiring varying degrees of humidity, so choose something that fits your conditions as nearly as possible.

It's a good idea to provide some humidity artificially in a centrally heated house – not just for the plants, but for the preservation of the furniture and for your own comfort. You can buy small ceramic water containers made to hang on the radiator, but better still are the electric humidifiers now available.

These will help, but for those plants that like it steamy, it's as well to provide even more. First of all, spray around the plants with a very fine spray of clear water. This will help a bit but, since it really needs to be done several times a day, it's certainly not the answer for the busy person. Let's face it, it's very hard to remember to spray a plant even if you have the time. Much better try to provide a local humidity more or less permanently.

37 Hand spray all round the plant

38 Provide extra humidity by putting the plant pot in a larger container packed with peat or sphagnum moss which should be kept wet

39 Stand the pot on a layer of pebbles almost covered in water – but be careful not to drown the roots

Grouping plants together goes a long way towards this. The water vapour given off by the plants from their leaves tends to become trapped underneath and amongst the other leaves to the plants' mutual benefit.

You can provide a little microclimate by putting the plant pot into a decorative container several sizes too big for it. Pack between the pots with peat or sphagnum moss and keep it wet. As the water evaporates, it will provide extra humidity around the plant.

Much the same effect can be achieved by placing the pot into a tray of pebbles, almost covered in water. To avoid overwatering and 'drowning' the roots, never allow the water level to come above the bottom of the pot.

I like to combine the benefits of the pebble tray with the plant grouping idea by using a large tray and positioning several pots onto it with more or less the tallest in the middle with the others grouped around.

Even more humid conditions can be achieved by growing plants in large carboys or in a fishtank or one of those very posh 'Wardian cases' – which are like miniature Victorian conservatories and very attractive (and expensive) indeed. More of that later.

Watering

Now this is the knottiest problem of them all, and I have to admit one that is not at all easy to advise on. The only real truth is that plants should be watered when they need it. Knowing when that is is the secret of success and such timing varies from plant to plant.

To make matters worse, it's not too easy to tell whether

a plant is suffering because it's short of water or because it doesn't have enough. Alas, the symptoms are exactly the same. What happens when a plant is overwatered is that the tiny root hairs, which are responsible for absorbing water from the soil, rot off, making it impossible for the plant to take up more. So it wilts and looks for all the world as if it needs more water. Mind you, if you do give it more it won't do much harm because by that time it's generally too late anyway.

So, you just have to give your plants a great deal of attention: look at them often and worry a bit about them until you get used to how much they need – and those green fingers of yours will tell you a considerable amount, too, so use them often.

The best way to decide whether or not the compost is dry is to feel it. Just rub a tiny bit of compost between thumb and forefinger and you'll be able to feel quite accurately whether or not water is needed. Naturally the amount you allow the compost to dry varies from plant to plant. An azalea should never become bone dry, so water it when the top of the compost feels just moist. A mother-in-law's tongue, on the other hand, can be allowed to dry almost to dust between waterings.

Whichever the plant is, however much water it requires, the rules are the same. Never give it a little water every day, or even once a week, regardless. Some houseplant growers have a watering day once a week when they do everything. Others forget to water for weeks and then soak them all, while a few conscientious liberals treat them like their children and give them a watering three times a day after meals. None is correct.

Do look at them every day and do feel the compost every day, at least until you get used to their requirements. When you have decided that the compost is dry enough for more water, give the pot a real soaking, allow it to drain and then leave it alone until it dries out again.

The easiest way to water, in my opinion, is to dump the whole plant in the kitchen sink and hold it underwater until bubbles stop rising. Then you can be certain that the compost is thoroughly soaked. Then leave it on the draining board for a few minutes to allow the excess to drain away before putting it back in its saucer.

However, this is not the best way for that enormous rubber plant that's pushing its way through the ceiling!

40 Test the compost for dryness by rubbing between your thumb and forefinger

41 The simplest way to water small plants is to stand them in the kitchen sink

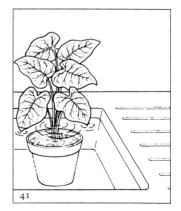

42 Some plants should be watered from below by standing them in a tray of water

43 Water plants which demand an acid compost with cold tea to neutralise the lime in chalky water

That will have to be watered with a can from above. All you have to do is to fill the pot with water, wait a while and do it again until you can see a bit coming out at the bottom. Then you know you've soaked the compost. It's worth noting here that, when you pot a plant into a larger pot, you must leave enough room at the top for watering.

An alternative watering technique is to water plants from below, and there are two methods. The commonest is simply to stand the pot in a tray of water and allow it to suck up water by capillary action. Wait for a minute or two until you can see tiny drops of water on the surface telling you that the compost is thoroughly soaked. This is a good way to water plants, such as African violets, whose leaves are damaged by water. Cyclamen benefit, too, because it avoids getting water into the concave top of the corm which could then rot.

The second method of watering from below is to stand the pots on small pads of absorbent material, which are kept moist all the time. You can use a piece of old carpet underfelt or you can buy special mats that are impregnated with fertiliser too. This is, on a much smaller scale, the way the commercial growers water most of their plants. Plants have to be in plastic pots and potted in soilless compost for this method to work well. In theory, the plant takes up as much water as it requires but in practice it doesn't quite work like that because the compost is kept constantly moist. For those plants that need constant moisture it's ideal, but plants that like drier conditions are better watered in the traditional way. Mind you, it's an excellent method of watering when you go away on holiday.

Just two points about the water itself. It's never a good idea to treat plants harshly or to shock them, so drenching the roots with icy water is to be avoided. Just take the chill off the water before use.

Some plants, notably azaleas and ericas, must not be watered with chalky tap water. They demand an acid compost, and watering continually with water that contains chalk would eventually make the compost alkaline. So in this case, instead of using plain water, use cold tea. The tannic acid is just enough to neutralise the lime in the water.

Feeding

All plants grown in pots must rely on the grower for their food, so regular feeding is essential. However, it is possible to overfeed pot plants, resulting in scorched leaves and poor growth, so a little care is needed. It certainly doesn't follow that the more feed you pump into a plant the better it will grow.

Plants require three main elements: nitrogen for leaf and stem growth; phosphorus for healthy root growth; and potassium for the development of flowers and fruit. So it's easy to see that foliage plants would benefit from a fertiliser high in nitrogen to encourage the growth of the leaves, while flowering plants would need more potassium for flower production.

Unfortunately, most houseplant fertilisers fail to differentiate between the two types of plant. They generally take the middle road to provide one feed that will do for all types of plant. That is certainly the most convenient way and will give quite adequate results. However, for the houseplant enthusiast who is after perfection, I would recommend a different system.

The normal run-of-the-mill fertiliser has nitrogen, phosphorus and potassium in equal quantities, normally in the ratio of 7:7:7 or twice as strong at 14:14:14. This is perfectly good for normal use but is too low in potassium for flowering plants and too low in nitrogen for the best foliage. Much better use a tomato fertiliser, which is high in potassium for the flowering types, and a general garden feed high in nitrogen for the foliage types.

Liquid feeding is the most common method, and such a form acts faster than a solid granular fertiliser, but has a shorter working life. If you care for your plants and can remember to feed regularly, then this is the method that gives most control.

If you're a bit disorganised and find it difficult to remember to feed, then a slow-release fertiliser is for you. This is a granular type that is activated to release its nutrients to the plant roots only when the compost is warm and wet. Thus it lets out a slow but steady stream of plant food as it's required in the summer. All you have to do is to remember to feed about once a quarter. The danger here, of course, is that after the first feed the plants could be forgotten entirely.

Symptoms of mismanagement

- Leaves brown particularly at tips – too much light;

- Leaves wilt in sunlight   too much light or over- or under-watering;

- Weak, spindly growth – too little light;

- Flowers falling – lack of humidity;

- Variegated leaves turn green – too little light;

- Edges of leaves turn brown – over- or under-watering;

- Leaves turn yellow between veins – lack of nutrients;

- Leaves turn yellow all over – lack of nutrients or over- or under-watering;

- Brown spots on leaves – over- or under-watering or nutrient deficiency;

- Fungus growth on leaves and stems – humidity too high or temperature too low;

- Leaves turn red – low temperature;

- Too much leaf and little flower growth – overfeeding.

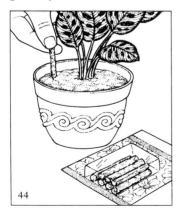

44 Fertiliser sticks are pushed into the compost around the plant to release the nutrients gradually

44

Another long-lasting method that is relatively new in the United Kingdom is fertiliser sticks. These are simply pushed into the compost around the plant; the water gradually dissolves them to release the nutrients. They seem to work very well, although I retain the same reservations as for other slow-release fertilisers.

Foliar feeding is a very fast way to make plants absorb and use nutrients. This special fertiliser is sprayed onto the leaves, where it is absorbed. This is an ideal method, then, of taking fast action when deficiencies are noticed. As you would expect, the effect is short-lived so it's necessary to liquid feed at the same time.

Timing of the feeding programme is important. You

should never feed plants when they are more or less resting during the winter. If you try to force them along, growth will be weak and spindly and the general vigour of the plant will decrease. Give them a holiday in the winter, and they'll work hard for you during the summer when you're on yours. The one exception to this rule is if you have tropical plants growing with artificial heat and light. They should be kept growing all the time.

It's quite easy to overfeed houseplants in the mistaken belief that it will do them good. It doesn't, so you should stick to the rules. Feed only when the plants are in full growth. Don't feed for a couple of months after repotting or after buying a new plant. There will be enough fertiliser in the compost to last that long. Never add a bit extra for luck. The instructions on the bottle should always be adhered to. Indeed it's better to err on the side of weakness than the other way around.

Some commercial growers are now putting slow-release fertilisers into their composts in order to save their customers feeding for about six months. Unfortunately, there seems to be no indication on the label that this is so. In this case, it's as well to ask when you buy.

Repotting
Plants growing in pots need a change of compost or extra compost each year. Because of constant watering and feeding, the compost is likely to become sour and inhospitable to roots, or it may simply be exhausted.

Plants growing in pots naturally fill their space quite quickly and, when they do, it's essential to provide more compost for them to continue growing. This necessitates a larger pot.

The time to repot is in the spring just as the plant starts into new growth. Never repot in the winter because the roots will not be actively growing at that time, so you would simply be surrounding the roots with cold, wet compost and very few plants will thank you for cold feet. Repot flowering plants when they finish flowering.

Give the plant a good watering and knock it out of the pot by turning it upside down and knocking the edge of the pot on the side of a table. Then have a look at the rootball. If there are few roots showing, return the plant to its pot and wait a while. There is no value in repotting too soon, that is before the roots are running around the

45 Put the old pot into the new one on top of a layer of compost. Then fill round with compost, working it down with a pencil

46 Repot a fuchsia into a smaller pot to encourage flowering. Tease out the old compost from between the roots with a plant label

bottom of the pot and almost completely covering the compost ball.

Always pot into the container the next size up. It's a mistake to try to save a stage by potting into a container that's too large. You'll then surround the roots with compost that will remain cold and inhospitable, and, without roots to aerate it, the new compost will soon pack down and turn sour. Mind you, when you use a pot the next size up, it's not easy to work fresh compost down between the rootball and the side of the pot without causing damage – not easy that is, unless you know how.

Start by putting a little compost into the bottom of the new pot and then set the old pot on top of it. Fill around the sides with compost, working it down with a pencil. Don't, however, compact it too hard. A knock on the bench from time to time is generally enough to consolidate the compost sufficiently. When the compost has been packed around right to the top, the old pot can be removed.

You'll then find that the new pot has a complete lining of compost just the correct size to take the rootball. Simply place the plant in its new home, tap the pot on the bench and the job's done. Give the plant a good watering in and then don't water again until the compost dries out.

Some flowering plants, such as fuchsias, will flower better in smaller pots. If their home is made too comfortable they become fat and idle, making masses of leaf and shoot growth at the expense of the flowers. So these plants are always potted into the same size pot. Some enthusiasts even pot them into a size smaller from time to time. When the plant is removed, the old compost is teased out from between the roots with a piece of wood. Then, with the rootball made smaller, the plant can be repotted in the normal way, back into the pot it came from.

Of course, there comes a time when it simply isn't practical to repot. Plants that have outgrown their space take a bit of shifting, let alone repotting! In this case, carefully scrape a couple of inches of compost from the top of the pot and replace it with new. The young roots will soon grow into it.

Pruning and training

There are various reasons for pruning houseplants, but it is mainly done to improve the look of the plant or to encourage new growth.

However green-fingered you may be, it would be remarkable if the odd leaf didn't die off some time or the tips didn't turn brown. Once this browning occurs, there's no point at all in keeping the leaf. It will not be able to add anything to the plant either by making food or by enhancing its looks, and once brown it certainly won't recover. It might just as well come off before it encourages fungus diseases, which may then spread to living tissue.

Scissors are the best tool for trimming and tidying up. If it's the tips that have gone, cut back almost to the end of the brown area, but not quite. If you cut into the green, the leaf will continue to turn brown further back. If it's a whole leaf or a stem that is affected, cut right back to its base.

This cleaning-up operation should go on all the time, so that the plants are kept looking attractive and the risk of spreading disease is reduced to a minimum. Sometimes even more drastic remedial action is necessary, and this takes not only an implement stronger than a pair of scissors but also the courage of a Cossack!

In the wild, some plants are quite content to lose their lower leaves, as long as those on the top remain intact. They generally grow amongst other plants, so they push their stems to the sky and that small tuft of leaves on the top is sufficient to soak up the necessary sunshine. Plants, such as rubber plants and *Dieffenbachia*, may grow long, lanky stems with just a topknot of leaves. That may be suitable for the jungle but it's not on in the front room.

Inspect the plant closely and you'll find that there are still a number of buds sitting dormant at the base of the stem, where the old leaves grew. This is where the courage comes in. If the stem is cut right back hard to a point just above these buds, the plant will grunt a little but eventually it will send out a new set of shoots from the base. Do the job in the spring and cut back to 4–6in. (10–15cm.) above the base of the plant. With some plants, such as the rubber plant, it's possible to air layer the top as an insurance policy, as suggested on page 13.

With most plants, this kind of drastic cutting back can be avoided by a system of regular pruning. If shoots are cut back, they will normally respond by sending out a couple of side shoots near where they have been cut. So, if you want to make a plant really bushy, you keep pinching back the side shoots.

47 Cut back lanky plants in the spring to 4–6 in. (10–15cm.) above the base

48 To make a bushy plant you should keep pinching back the side shoots

47

48

This pinching back is done when the shoots are green and soft and it's done with the fingernails. It's best to start when the plant is quite young and really to have a look each time you pass and, where you see a side shoot growing out a bit more vigorously than the others, pinch it off. It seems a poor return for extra effort, but there's no room for sentiment.

Even with regular pinching back, some plants will still manage to grow out of shape, sending out long errant shoots where they're not meant to be. Other plants are just not suited to pinching. In either of these cases, it may be necessary to shape the plant by cutting back thicker shoots. This is best done just as the plants are beginning to grow again in the spring. Use a pair of secateurs and cut back to a point just above a bud. Remember that the new growth will grow in the direction the bud is facing, so you should be able to visualise where the new shoot will grow.

The living room is obviously somewhat restricted, so it's necessary to contain the rampant growth of some plants, especially those that are climbing plants in the wild. Some pruning may be necessary but often it's best to train the plant in the position you wish it to grow. Naturally you'll need some sort of support to tie it to and there are plenty to choose from. Your garden centre or florist will be able to sell you all sorts from a straightforward garden cane to a tortuous contraption in split cane or plastic.

Some plants grow quite fast, but you should try to keep on top of the job, starting when it's young and tying in regularly. It's very easy to damage plants that have grown too much to be easily handled.

Pulling down branches has the effect of restricting the sap and this, in turn, will induce the plant to flower. It's a method often used with plants such as jasmine and *Stephanotis*. The plants can be trained round and round in a circle by tying them in regularly to a wire frame. It is possible to buy circular wire frames but it's considerably cheaper to make your own. Nothing could be simpler. Take a piece of 12 gauge wire, preferably plastic coated, bend it into a hoop, and stick the two ends into the pot. The plant can then be carefully tied to it in a circle.

A good way of training plants with aerial roots is with a moss stick. Buy some sphagnum moss from the florist and tie it to a cane. Then push the aerial roots into the stick

49 Tie climbing plants to a frame, starting when they're young to avoid damage

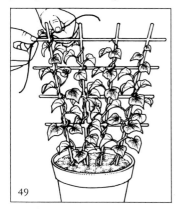

49

where possible and keep the moss moist by regular spraying. This will also increase humidity.

50 Jasmines are trained round a circular frame. Make your own from plastic-coated 12 gauge wire

51 Carefully tie the plant to the frame in a circle

52 Plants with aerial roots should be trained to a moss stick. Keep the moss moist by regular spraying to increase humidity

Stephanotis

53 Wipe leaves down with a damp sponge from time to time

Leaf cleaning

Plants breathe through their leaves and it's vital that these pores should not become clogged with dust. (Of course I know your house never sees a speck of dust but you must excuse me while I advise this for the other feller!)

In the wild, there is not much fine dust about and, where it does settle, it's soon washed off by rain. In the house we have to spring-clean regularly. Plain clear water makes an excellent job of cleaning leaves. Just wipe them down with a damp sponge from time to time. However, if you want a perfect shine, you'll have to use something other than plain water. There are several leaf-shine materials available, but not all are thoroughly safe for all plants in my view and in any case, they're relatively expensive. I use plain cows' milk and I find it shines leaves just as well.

Care after flowering

Most perennial plants will produce plenty of flowers, often on a bigger plant in the second year, provided they are built up and, in some cases, rested before they have to start again. However, it's no good expecting perennials to perform year after year unless you give them enough help and encouragement to build themselves up for the effort of flowering. This should start as soon as they have finished flowering and go on right through the season until they're ready to begin flowering again.

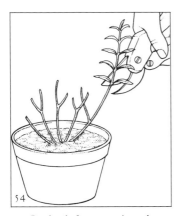

54 Cut back fast-growing plants such as winter cherry hard after flowering

Most shrubby plants, such as azaleas, require little or no pruning. Simply remove the spent flower heads as soon as possible to prevent the plants from wasting energy making seed. Then give them a good feed and put them outside in the garden once all danger of frost has passed. Remember that they have to be kept constantly moist and in a shady spot. The best place is under the dappled shade of trees or near to a large shrub. Feed them with a liquid fertiliser once a fortnight and water with rainwater to maintain acid conditions in the compost. Bring them inside again before the first frosts in October or November.

If you don't have a garden, put the plants in the coolest room you have but in a sunny spot. Remember that light levels are much lower in a house, so although they must be kept out of direct sunlight, they will need quite a bright place to live.

Some softer, faster-growing plants, such as winter cherry

(*Solanum capsicastrum*), should be cut hard back after flowering and then treated in much the same way.

Bulbs must be allowed to build up a flower for next year, though any that have been specially prepared for Christmas flowering are rarely worth bothering with. It's unlikely that they'll flower in the second year so, after they've finished flowering, they're best planted out into the garden where they'll slowly recover and flower a few years later.

Those that haven't been tampered with are a much better bet. Ideally, take them out of their bowls and put them in a sunny spot in the garden with the bulbs in a trench just covered with soil. Give them a good feed with a fertiliser high in potash – for example, a tomato feed – and they'll probably flower for you again when they are potted up again in August or September.

If you don't have a garden, they should be treated like other bulbous or tuberous plants that need a rest – begonias and amaryllis (*Hippeastrum*) are good examples. After flowering, they should be fed in the same way to build up the flowers for next year. After a while, they'll tell you when they are ready for their rest by turning brown at the tips of the leaves and looking generally tired. Stop feeding and start gradually to give them less water until you are not watering at all. By this time the foliage will have died right down. Clean up the bulb and put the pot somewhere where it won't get watered until it's time to start it into growth again.

Holiday care

Unless you're prepared to suffer a few losses, often because of over-zealous watering, it simply isn't fair to your neighbours to ask them to care for your plants while you're away for a fortnight or more. For the sake of good relations it's often best to be self-reliant.

The trick is to equalise the conditions as much as possible. Even though your plants may need full sun, put them in a room where they won't get direct sunlight, along with the shade lovers. The room should be not too hot nor too cold.

Watering is, of course, the problem. The best bet is to put the plants in the bathroom, actually in the bath. Stand them on a bath towel, one end of which is dipped into a bucket or bowl of water. The water will pass by capillary

55 Stand the plants in the bath on a towel kept wet in a bucket of water

55

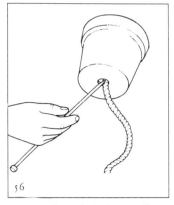

56 Use a large knitting needle to push a capillary wick through the drainage hole of a clay pot

action through the towel and the plants will suck up the water as they need it. That works with plastic pots in soilless compost but not if the pots are clay, in which case you'll have to buy a capillary wick from a garden centre or cut a few lengths off your pyjama cord. Push the wicks up through the drainage hole with a large knitting needle so that they are well into the compost with a length poking out. They will act as a transport channel for water. Naturally it would take a worry off your mind if you asked a neighbour to come in to fill up the bucket from time to time.

If even that is impossible, you'll have to reduce the plants' need for water. First of all, spray all the plants with a combined insecticide/fungicide to prevent the spread of pest problems. Then put each one into a polythene bag with an elastic band around the pot and then stand the pots on the towel. Better still, buy a proprietary holiday bag, which will breathe just a little. The effect is to inhibit the loss of water through the leaves and thus restrict the plants' need for more.

Winter holidays are a much bigger problem. If you intend to turn off the central heating, you'll either have to give the plants to a friend or relative to look after or take them with you!

PESTS AND DISEASES

Houseplants are as prone to attack from pests and diseases as are the plants in the garden. However, because of the equable conditions inside the house, any plant disorders are likely to multiply and spread much faster. So, keep an eagle eye open and act as soon as you see anything amiss.

Often the first line of defence is simply to remove the pest with your fingers and squash it. This is not the most pleasant job but such action could nip the trouble in the bud. It's the same with diseases. As soon as you see the first sign, remove the offending leaf and burn it or put it in the dustbin.

If the attack persists, chemicals will inevitably have to be resorted to. If you do spray, do it outside on a calm day. If you must stay inside, put the plant in a dustbin bag and spray it in that. Chemical insecticides and fungicides are not only dangerous in enclosed spaces but can cause nasty stains on the furniture. Don't necessarily jump to the conclusion that it's a disease that is attacking an ailing plant. Check this list of disorders first of all.

57

57 Protect yourself and your furniture from chemical insecticides by spraying inside a dustbin bag

---

Plant disorders

Yellowing leaves
Caused either by over- or underwatering, bad light conditions, draughts or a nutrient deficiency. If the yellowing is restricted to the area between the veins, then a nutrient deficiency is almost certain.

Brown leaves
Again, over- or underwatering, draughts, sun-scorch, dry air or over- or under-feeding could be the cause.

Spots on the leaves
Could be sun-scorch, especially if the plant has been sprayed with water or insecticide when it has been in bright sunlight. It could also be due to a nutrient deficiency or to our old friend the watering can.

Loss of variegation
Some variegated plants will quite naturally revert to green and the remedy is simple: just cut off the green shoots. However, if the plant is in the wrong light conditions it could also be the cause of greening up.

Leaf and flower bud dropping
Often due to lack of humidity or to the plant having been subjected to low temperatures at some time. It could also, like most other disorders, be due to faulty watering.

Non flowering
Often caused by good foliage and stem growth so that the plant has no need to flower and make seed. Non flowering can be remedied by reducing watering and stopping feeding. Bear in mind too that some plants will flower only when light conditions, particularly day length, are correct.

Thin growth
Due to lack of light.

Wilting
Caused by sudden bright sunshine or by over- or underwatering.

Pests
Aphids
Greenfly and blackfly will attack almost everything, generally clustering at the soft shoot tips and sucking the sap. They also make a sticky substance called honeydew, which is much loved by ants, so aphids should be removed. Often this can be done by simply wiping them or by washing them off under the tap. Alternatively spray all but poinsettias with an insecticide containing *permethrin*.

Whitefly
Not quite so common as aphids but a real nuisance if you get a visitation. You can't kill the eggs and the whitefly has a very short life cycle. So, though you may get rid of the adults with one spraying, the eggs will soon hatch and, unless you spray them before they start their courting, you'll have another batch of eggs, and so it goes on.

The answer is to spray a second time within no more than seven days from the first. Again, use *permethrin*, except on poinsettias.

Red spider mite

A tiny mite that it's really impossible to see with the naked eye. You'll see them as a hazy red cloud hanging from leaves if the infestation is bad, and the leaves will take on a silvery, bleached look. Spray the plants with water regularly to keep red spider mites at bay since they don't like damp conditions. If the worst comes to the worst, spray with *malathion* or *dimethoate*, but check the bottle first to ensure that it won't damage the plant.

Scale insects

Sap suckers cling to leaves and build a protective scale around themselves, which makes them difficult to control. They generally cluster under leaves where their activities soon distort and disfigure the foliage. If the infestation is small, they can be prised off with your fingernail, but, if there are too many, spray with *dimethoate* or *malathion*.

Caterpillars

Now these are really delightful creatures who can be excused for getting in with the wrong crowd. They vandalise plants by eating holes in the leaves, but bear in mind that they'll change into rather attractive butterflies or moths. So, if you can bear to, pick them off the leaves and put them outside where they'll not do much damage. If you're bent on revenge, spray with *dimethoate*.

Leaf miners

The moles of the insect world, these creatures burrow into leaves and make quite distinct and disfiguring trails of yellow lines where they have burrowed. They are especially common on cinerarias and chrysanthemums. Spray with *dimethoate*.

Vine weevils

If your plant collapses for no apparent reason, suspect vine weevil. Knock the plant out of the pot and look for small white maggots. If you see them, water the compost with *permethrin*.

Fungus gnats

These tiny flies lay their eggs on the surface of the compost. The grubs hatch out and burrow downwards, feeding on the organic matter in the compost and damaging roots in the process. Control them by watering with *permethrin*.

Mealy bug
These bugs, which look like little pads of cotton wool, are sap-sucking insects that cover themselves with a white, waxy coating. Remove them by painting with *methylated spirits* or by spraying with *dimethoate*.

Thrips
These small flies live on the undersides of leaves and are very mobile. They suck sap and disfigure leaves, and can be detected by distortion and scratches on the leaf surface. Control with *permethrin*.

Diseases
Fungus diseases can be controlled with *thiophanate-methyl* or *propiconazole* fungicides. Viruses, however, are incurable.

Mildew
This is a white, powdery mould generally caused by the plants being too wet and under-ventilated. Pick off diseased leaves, reduce watering, increase ventilation and spray with either fungicide.

Botrytis
A grey, fluffy mould appears on stems, leaves and flowers generally on soft tissue. It is caused by low temperatures and too much moisture. Avoid watering and overhead spraying and increase temperatures. Remove infected leaves and spray with fungicide.

Damping off
This fungus attacks young seedlings, which keel over owing to the stems rotting at ground level. Sow thinly, increase ventilation, remove infected seedlings and water with fungicide.

Sooty mould
This black fungus grows on the sticky excretion of aphids. Wipe it off with soapy water and spray against aphids.

Rust
Causes yellow patches on the surface of the leaves with matching brown pustules underneath. Spray all house-plants except fuchsias with *propiconazole*.

Virus diseases
These cause a wide range of different symptoms from discoloration to quite severe distortion of leaves. There is no cure so plants should be isolated from others until you're sure it really is a virus disease when it should be thrown away. The diseases are transmitted by aphids, which must be controlled as soon as you see them.

SPECIAL DISPLAYS

Most houseplants are grown and displayed separately, standing either on the floor, the windowsill or a shelf with perhaps the one concession to art being a decorative pot cover. Not desperately imaginative.

On the other hand, we've all been impressed by those dramatic displays of houseplants you can sometimes see in offices, hotels or restaurants. Large groups, dominated perhaps by two or three enormous foliage plants, complemented by smaller groups of foliage in a variety of colours and leaf shapes and brightened up by a few flowering subjects. They look good and there's no doubt they grow better.

Of course we can't do anything quite that ambitious in the front room or we may have to hire native bearers to find the television set, but the idea is as good in the home as it is in an office block. As I've mentioned before, because they help each other maintain a humid atmosphere, plants will always fare better in the company of others, and they'll look much more natural too.

Choosing the plants

If you're going to grow plants in a group, it's essential to choose those that like similar conditions. It's never going to work if you mix the shade lover with the sun worshipper or the tropical native with the alpine. Think carefully about temperature and position first. Then, if you intend to take plants out of their pots and grow them together in the same compost in a communal container, you'll also have to ensure that they all require much the same watering regime. Every year at Christmas time you'll be able to buy bowls of plants made up by the growers. Many of them will not be seeing another Christmas, because the plant combination is a disaster. At that time, I'll guarantee that you could find in any shop a bowl containing a chrysanthemum and an azalea – one a lover of dry conditions and the other of moisture. You'll see a cyclamen rubbing shoulders with a maranta, representing the two extremes of the temperature range. So be careful or buy plants separately and pot them into the bowls yourself.

In the section describing the plants you'll find them already classified into those that require certain conditions. When choosing plants to grow together, take them out of one section only and check their watering requirements if you intend to put them together.

Multiple planting

Plants can simply be grouped together to make an attractive display in a decorative bowl, tub or wooden trough. If the peat is kept moist, watering will be reduced and water will constantly evaporate around the plants creating the humid atmosphere they require. By keeping the plants in their pots, the roots are contained, so effectively reducing the rate of growth, and they can be watered and fed separately according to their needs.

This method has the advantage that, when a plant in the display needs replacing, it can simply be removed without disturbing the others. Its disadvantage is that watering and feeding are awkward because pots are hidden – there's even a danger of missing the watering of a pot altogether.

The alternative method of multiple planting is to take the plants out of their pots, fill the container with potting compost and set all the plants direct in that. The roots will then have a larger volume of compost to grow in so the growth rate should be faster – perhaps even too fast! Naturally, if you do it this way, it's imperative to ensure that all the plants require the same amount of water and feed. There's also a bit of a disadvantage in that plants that need replacing are difficult to remove without damaging other roots.

Whichever method you decide to follow, there are a few rules to observe. Obviously there are artistic considerations like positioning the tallest plants at the back. But bear in mind that light levels have to be taken into account and this will affect the make-up of the group. Shade lovers, in other words, can be planted with sun lovers provided they are given the shade of a taller plant between them and the source of light.

It may seem that there are so many variables to take into account that choosing compatible plants is impossible. However, plants do like growing together and if they are, they'll put up with slightly less than perfect conditions quite happily. The choice is likely to be wider than you think.

58 Fill a decorative container with potting compost for an attractive display of several plants – but make sure they all require the same amount of water and feed

58

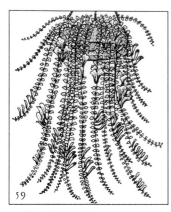

59

59 Hanging baskets are a popular way of displaying plants

Hedera

There is one danger in growing plants together in the same compost and that is drainage. A large tub or a trough must have a solid bottom. If it has holes in it, water will seep out and rot the carpet! If you can find a drip tray large enough to go under a tub, that's ideal and you should bore holes in the bottom of the tub. However, if you have, for example, a trough on legs, catching the water isn't easy, so drainage holes can't really be provided. Therefore, before filling the container with compost, put a layer of gravel in the bottom and be very, very careful that you never over-water.

Hanging baskets

Plants in hanging baskets are becoming fashionable now for a strange reason. Because of rising fuel prices, growers have been anxiously looking for ways to cut their oil, gas and coal bills. One way to do that is to put more plants in the greenhouse so, when stagings are full, many growers have resorted to filling the roof space with plants growing in hanging containers.

Shops have therefore become filled with more hanging baskets than ever and growers have been busy encouraging us to buy them. That's no bad thing because they really do look good, and they can fill a space where there's no other way of accommodating a plant.

It seems silly, but fixing a hook into the ceiling can cause problems. In old houses, the ceiling often consists of straw or some material, covered in plaster. In this case, you'll have to pierce it with a thin bradawl until you find a beam underneath to screw the hook into.

In modern houses, the ceiling is invariably made with plasterboard nailed to the ceiling timbers and plastered over. Here you can do the same thing as for older houses, finding and fixing to a beam, or you can use a special fixing. The do-it-yourself shop will stock a little gadget that you can poke through a small hole in the plasterboard. When pushed fully through, two spring-loaded 'wings' open out behind the board to hold the hook firmly.

You can buy hanging baskets already made up but, better still, make your own basket. Unlike those that you might use outside, indoor hanging baskets must be fully enclosed to prevent water dripping on the carpet. Sizes range from those made to take a single pot to one that will hold an arrangement of three or four plants.

If you simply put a potted plant into a decorative hanging container, it's important to take care with the watering. The container will probably be hanging too high for you to see how much water goes into the pot and you certainly won't be able to see how much comes out of the bottom. This means that the pot could finish up standing in water in the container and that spells certain death. So the best bet is to remove the pot completely, submerge it in the sink of water and allow it to drain fully before replacing it.

Naturally, you should choose plants that are seen at their best in the hanging position – either those that trail or flowering plants whose flowers hang down, making them best viewed from below.

Plants for hanging baskets

For cool rooms
Asparagus sprengeri, Browallia, Campanula isophylla, Chlorophytum, Cissus, Hedera, Philodendron scandens, Saxifraga stolonifera, Tolmiea, Tradescantia and *Zebrina*.

For warm rooms
Achimenes longiflora, Begonia vars, *Columnea, Ficus pumila, Nephrolepis* and *Plectranthus*.

Left: *Tradescantia*
Above: *Ficus pumila*

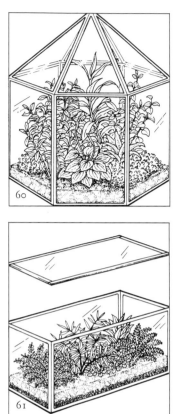

60 The Wardian case, or miniature greenhouse, beloved by Victorians, is making a welcome comeback

61 A fishtank makes a less expensive, but quite as successful, container for small plants

Indoor greenhouses

One of the continual problems with many houseplants is the maintenance of a level of humidity high enough for healthy growth. Tropical plants, which grow in the steamy jungle, will never be really at home in the dry atmosphere of a modern house and even some of those, such as ferns, that can tolerate lower temperatures won't be at their best in dry air. One of the most effective ways of ensuring that plants have a humid atmosphere around them is to provide them with a closed 'greenhouse' in the front room.

In the Victorian era, when the craze for ferns was at its height, the 'Wardian case' achieved fashionable popularity. There were many types, but generally they were miniature replicas of those wonderfully elaborate Victorian conservatories that adorned most stately homes – and indeed, still do. They were normally filled with ferns, watered regularly and ventilated quite irregularly to entrap the evaporating water. They worked extremely well and they looked very attractive. So, it's good to see that the old-fashioned Wardian case is making a comeback.

Garden centres and florists now stock a whole range of these miniature greenhouses, which will make a very fine ornamental piece in the sitting room. All you have to do is to position it in a fairly shady spot, put a little moist peat or moss in the bottom and stand your humidity lovers inside. Then close the lid until they need attention. There's the inevitable snag – they're not cheap.

However, for me the plants, not the container, are the main interest, so there's no need to spend a fortune on anything quite so elaborate. A fishtank makes a very acceptable container for small plants and it won't cost so much. To retain the humidity, seal the top with a sheet of glass. For safety, the glass should either be set in a wooden frame such as a picture-frame or have the edges protected with strong tape.

As well as standing pots in the containers, plants can also be grown direct in compost. However, be warned: watering can be tricky with no drainage holes, so don't overdo it.

In the garden centre or florist you will be able to find a good range of small plants especially for planting in a glass container, but bear in mind that their growth rate is likely to be faster than normal, so allow plenty of space.

To plant up a Wardian case, start with a layer of

drainage in the container. Coarse grit will do, but it's perhaps even better to use charcoal broken up into pieces about the size of a 5p piece. If you can't find anything suitable in the garden centre, use barbecue charcoal and break it up yourself and that's a nice messy job, believe me.

Then fill the container up to about 4in. (10cm.) with a soilless compost, knock the plants out of their pots and plant them directly into it. Water them in and replace the lid. From then on you'll find that the plants will need very little extra water. As the water evaporates, it condenses on the top of the glass and runs back into the compost, so it's a perfect recycling process. You'll need to keep an eye on the plants and water them if they look dry and perhaps re-move the top glass to ventilate them if they look too wet. It's a fairly fine balance that takes a bit of getting used to.

Bottle gardens

Almost any container that's big enough can be used to make a bottle garden. A sweet jar standing on its side will make quite an attractive feature but, for the real McCoy, there's nothing to beat a carboy.

If you can find one that was originally used for distilled water and could, ten years ago, be bought for a few bob from the garage, so much the better. They're few and far between now, I'm afraid, but you can buy something similar from the garden centre. The opening is likely to be a bit wider, which somewhat reduces the challenge, but plants will grow in them just as well.

There are also a few plastic containers made for planting, some even with lights in the top, but I can't work up a great deal of enthusiasm for them. The trouble is that when the water inside a bottle garden, or any other glass container, evaporates, it tends to mist up the sides. This is often a problem in the morning but the glass will clear as the bottle warms up during the day. In a glass container the condensation will trickle down, leaving the sides clear, but on plastic it tends to stick. Plastic containers with lighting in the top will heat up too much for the plants, so I think they're best left alone.

The way to plant a bottle garden is exactly the same as for an aquarium or a Wardian case, except that it has to be done through that narrow neck. You'll need special tools – all of which you can make yourself – and infinite patience because planting is a bit of a fiddle.

62 A carboy is the ideal container for a bottle garden

62

65

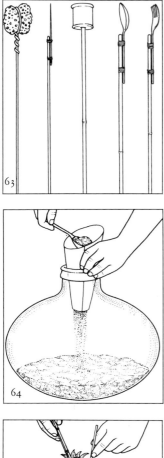

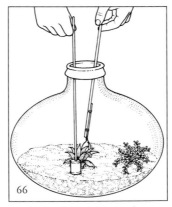

The 'spade' is made by tying a spoon onto a short garden cane; the 'fork' is a short cane attached to a table fork. The good old gardener's boot used to firm in after planting is a cotton reel on a cane. It's also useful to have a large darning needle mounted on a stick, as a sort of park-keeper's spike for spearing dead leaves and so on, and a piece of sponge or cloth to wipe the inside of the bottle. Fill the bottle by pouring the compost through a funnel improvised from cardboard.

Work out the planting pattern on a table by setting out the potted plants in a circle the size of the planting area in the bottle. Then make a hole with the spoon, remove the plant from its pot and spear it with the fork. Then lower it into the hole. You'll probably have to push it off with the cotton reel. Fill in around the plant and firm lightly with the cotton reel. Continue with the other plants in the same way.

When all the plants are in position, they must be watered. This is best done by gently pouring water down the side of the bottle. Done that way, you'll also wash off any compost that may be sticking to the sides. One easy way to do this is to use a pressure sprayer with the nozzle removed. However, do make sure you don't use too much water. At the risk of becoming boring, I think it's worth repeating the dangers of overwatering in a container without drainage holes. With too much water, the young roots will rot off and there will be a greatly increased risk of fungus diseases on the foliage and stems.

63 Tools for your bottle garden

64 Pour the compost through a cardboard funnel

65 Make a hole with the spoon

66 A cotton reel on a stick will firm the plants in lightly

67 Remove the nozzle from a sprayer to clean the compost from the sides of the bottle

Left: *Peperomia obtusifolia* 'variegata'

Below: *Maranta leuconeura* 'Kerchoveana'

If you do see any leaves affected by fungus, they must be removed immediately. If you can get your hand in the bottle, just nip them off with your thumb nail; otherwise cut them off with a razor blade stuck in the split end of a cane. (Such a dangerous tool must be handled very carefully.) The affected leaves can then be removed by spiking with the needle.

Feeding should be done with care. The growth rate of the plants will be pretty fast so, unless you fancy changing them regularly, try to limit growth a bit if you can. Feed only during the summer and then only about once a month.

Once you get the watering right, the bottle can be corked more or less all the time. However, if the compost looks very wet, remove the cork to ventilate the bottle and, if there's no condensation on the sides in the mornings, watering is needed. It takes a great deal of trial and error to get used to watering such containers.

The position of the bottle is important. Bear in mind that in a sunny window the temperature could soar inside the closed bottle, so make sure you never leave it in direct sunlight. The ideal spot is the happy medium where it will get a fair bit of sunlight but never so much that it is directly shining on that magnifying glass of a bottle.

Plants for bottle gardens

For closed bottles
Adiantum sp. (maidenhair ferns), *Asplenium* (bird's nest fern), *Chamaedorea elegans (syn. Neanthe bella)* (parlour palm), *Cryptanthus acaulis*, *Ficus pumila* (creeping fig), *Fittonia* (snakeskin plant), *Hedera helix* vars (ivy), *Maranta* (prayer plant), *Peperomia* sp. and *Selaginella* sp. (creeping moss).

For open bottles and containers
The above plants plus:
Cordyline terminalis, *Dieffenbachia compacta* (dumb cane), *Pilea* (aluminium plant) and *Sansevieria trifasciata* 'Hahnii' (bird's nest).

Alpine sinks

An unheated porch can be a difficult place to decorate. There's no doubt that the temperature inside will fall below freezing in the winter and, if it's glazed, there will be high temperatures and plenty of sun during the day.

In the summer, such a small enclosed place is not too difficult to fill because there will be no frost. You could use summer bedding plants potted into 3½in. (9cm.) pots. Petunias, salvias, geraniums, fuchsias and French marigolds, for example, will thrive provided they're fed and watered regularly. The winter is a different story.

The ideal plants for the winter are alpines. They will need no frost protection but they'll thank you for shelter from rain and they'll flower early and prolifically. While they can be displayed separately in pots, perhaps sunk to their rims in sand in a trough, they make a much finer display in a stone sink. Of course, pukka stone sinks are almost impossible to come by these days, but it's easy to make your own.

The mould is made with a couple of cardboard boxes,

68 You can improvise your own concrete trough for alpine displays. Make the mould from two cardboard boxes, and reinforce the bottom and sides with wire netting

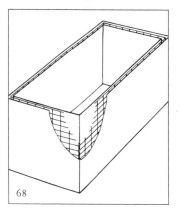

one smaller than the other, so that when it's put inside the larger one, the space between the two boxes will make the walls. These should be something like $1\frac{1}{2}$in. (4cm.) thick so you'll have to search the supermarket for boxes the right size.

Make the concrete with peat, builders' sand and cement. Use sphagnum moss peat and sieve it first, then mix $2\frac{1}{2}$ parts of sand with $1\frac{1}{2}$ parts of peat and 1 part of ordinary Portland cement. Mix it to a fairly sloppy consistency.

Start by putting a layer about $1\frac{1}{2}$in. (4cm.) thick in the bottom of the big box. Then cut four wooden pegs, about $1\frac{1}{2}$in. (4cm.) long from an old broomhandle or similar. The concrete will also need to be reinforced with wire netting, so cut a piece to fit the bottom of the larger box so it is big enough almost to reach the sides. Square mesh wire pea guards are ideal for reinforcing.

Push the reinforcing wire into the concrete so that it's roughly in the middle of the layer and then insert the pegs through the wire. Later on the pegs will be pushed out again to make drainage holes. Rest the smaller box on the four pegs and the concrete. Then cut some more reinforcing wire to fit around the smaller box, making it a bit larger than the box. In other words it should sit in the middle of the concrete walls when the mould is filled. Put the wire in place and fill the small box with bricks or sand to support the cardboard.

Now fill in between the two boxes with concrete, working it down to the bottom with a stick and tapping the sides of the larger box regularly to remove all air bubbles. When the gap is full, you'll find that you need to support the sides of the large box, too. This can be done by leaning a few paving slabs or bricks against it. The box will still distort but this is to be desired to give the worn, antique look, as if the sink had been carved from a solid block of stone as the originals actually were.

After twenty-four hours, remove the larger box. It should tear easily because it will be quite wet. Then add the 'well-used look': with an old wood chisel, round the edges and smooth the sides. Go over all of it with a soft brush to give a smooth finish and then leave it where it is for at least a week. It takes that long for the concrete to harden properly. Finally knock the pegs out of the bottom, and you'll have a trough that looks for all the world as if it were a hundred years old.

Viola alpina

The compost for alpines must be very well drained indeed, so I would mix good garden soil, peat and ⅛in. (3mm.) grit in equal quantities. Put a layer of broken clay pots or gravel in the bottom before filling.

Alpine plants suitable for a sink

Achillea, Albuca humilis, Androsace, Aquilegia discolor, Armeria, Betula nana, Calceolaria darwinii, Cytisus demissus, Dianthus, Draba, Euryops acraeus, Forsythia viridissima, Fuchsia procumbens, Gentiana, Geranium subcaulescens, Jasminum parkeri, Juniperus communis compressa, Leucojum roseum, Lewisia, Morisia monantha, Myrtus nummularia, Narcissus, Omphalodes luciliae, Phlox, Potentilla eriocarpa, Primula, Ramonda, Raoulia, Salix reticulata, Saxifraga, Sedum, Sempervivum, Thymus, Veronica, Viola.

After the alpines are planted, mulch over the top of the compost with grit to make an attractive finish and to keep the water away from the necks of the plants.

Alpines need absolutely minimal maintenance, but it's vital that they should never be overwatered. It's impossible to say exactly how much water they require, but think in terms of something like once a fortnight in the summer and once a month or six weeks in the winter. Alpines need no fertiliser unless they're not growing at all, when they could be given a weak liquid feed.

PLANTS FOR COLD ROOMS

These are the real toughies of the houseplant fraternity. Those recommended for a winter display will withstand temperatures from below freezing up to about 50°C (122°F). In other words, they would be perfectly at home in the garden. In the protection of the house, they'll generally flower earlier and the quality of the flowers and foliage should be better.

Hardy plants, however, are happiest when temperatures are low, so, if you do decide to bring them into a warmer room, perhaps when they're in flower, make it a temporary sojourn. In the summer, they would all be best outside where they'll recover in preparation for another winter inside.

Left: *Antirrhinum*
Below: *Aquilegia akitensis*

While the hardy plants are outdoors, they can be replaced with those plants recommended for a spring and a summer display. These are mainly annuals, which can be thrown away after use. They'll withstand temperatures from freezing point (which shouldn't occur in the summer anyway), up to about 16°C (60°F). Most require good light conditions and they should all be kept out of draughts, which will kill even the hardiest outdoor type.

Antirrhinum (Snapdragon)

A summer-flowering hardy annual that will make a fine, long-lasting houseplant. Choose F_1 hybrids of dwarf habit.

Sow in gentle heat from January to March and, when the seedlings are large enough to handle, transplant to $3\frac{1}{2}$in. (9cm.) pots. Feed with the high potash fertiliser after about six weeks, starting at half strength and increasing to full strength when the flower buds show. Keep the plants in full light and allow them to dry almost completely before rewatering.

Remove faded flowers to prolong the flowering period and discard these plants after flowering.

Aquilegia

A hardy perennial with superb, delicate foliage and exotic flowers in spring and summer. Choose a short variety like 'Dragonfly'.

Sow in gentle heat from January to March or lift a plant from the garden in October; alternatively, buy one from the garden centre. The plants should be potted into $3\frac{1}{2}$–4in. (9–10cm.) pots and fed with half-strength high potash fertiliser until the flower buds show, when full strength should be used. Keep in semi shade and water when the top of the compost feels just moist.

After flowering, the foliage is still worthwhile. It will die down in the autumn and this perennial should then be planted out in the garden.

Astilbe

Hardy perennial with superb divided foliage and great plumes of pink, yellow, rose and white flowers in the late spring and summer.

It can be raised from seed sown from January to March in gentle heat, but it's probably better to lift a plant from the garden or buy one from the garden centre, since it will take a year to reach flowering size.

Pot into 3½–4in. (9–10cm.) pots and feed with high potash fertiliser. Keep in semi shade and water when the compost feels just moist.

After flowering, retain the plant for the foliage. When it dies down plant it out in the garden.

Aucuba (Spotted Laurel)
A hardy shrub with shiny green foliage mottled and splashed with yellow.

It can be raised from softwood cuttings taken in June or bought from the garden centre. Feed with the balanced fertiliser recommended for foliage plants and keep in semi shade. Water when the top of the compost feels just moist.

It will benefit from a spell outside in the summer, though this is not essential.

Bulbs
I've included these all together because the cultivation details are identical for all spring-flowering types and similarly the summer-flowering kinds are all treated in the same way. For details of how to raise both types see pp. 21–3.

Bulb flowering seasons

Christmas flowering
Daffodils (prepared), hyacinths (prepared) and *Narcissus* 'Soleil d'Or' and 'Paperwhite'.

January flowering
Chionodoxa, crocus, hyacinths (unprepared) and snowdrops.

February flowering
Eranthis, Erythronium, Fritillaria and *Narcissus* (unprepared).

March flowering
Iris reticulata, Muscari, Ranunculus, Scilla and tulips.

April and May flowering
Ixia, Sparaxis, Triteleia, Tritonia and tulips.

Summer-flowering bulbs
Crinum, Eucomis, Ismene, Nerine and *Pleione*.

Above: *Narcissus* 'Soleil d'Or'

Right: *Muscari armeniacum*

All bulbs require a sunny spot but out of direct sunlight. Feed with the high potash fertiliser at half strength when in bud and flower and at full strength after flowering. When the flowers have faded, spring-flowering bulbs can be put outside in the garden during the summer. However, don't make the mistake of forgetting them after they have finished flowering or they'll be useless for next year. Continue to feed and water the leaves, even though you may want to put them out of the way to make room for something else more attractive. Once the foliage starts to turn brown, stop feeding and reduce the watering gradually until the bulbs are completely dry. Then store them until it's time for repotting.

Bulbs specially prepared for Christmas flowering cannot be forced again so they must be either thrown away or planted out in the garden where they'll flower again in perhaps two years' time.

Summer-flowering bulbs should also be watered and fed after flowering and dried off in the same way, though they are best left in their pots.

Darwin hybrid tulips

Campanula isophylla
This half-hardy perennial is the subject of a breeding breakthrough that gives us an exciting new plant. The new 'Kristal' varieties can be raised cheaply from seed sown in January or February in gentle heat. They'll flower in June right through the year until Christmas.

Pot into $3-3\frac{1}{2}$in. (7.5–9cm.) pots or in a hanging container. This perennial should be put in full light and given a half-strength potash feed once a fortnight. Allow the top of the compost to dry out almost completely between waterings.

Coleus (Flame Nettle)
A half-hardy perennial foliage plant available in a great variety of colour combinations. Sow in gentle heat at any time, bearing in mind that they are only suitable for cold rooms during the summer. So, for a room that may descend to frost in the winter, sow in March. However, if you can keep a temperature of 7°C (45°F) all year round, *Coleus* can be sown to give a succession of plants all year.

Pot into 3–3½in. (7.5–9cm.) pots, give them a semi-shaded spot and feed fortnightly with the general-purpose feed. Water when the top of the compost feels just moist.

The plants will produce insignificant flowers that are unattractive and will greatly reduce the quality of the foliage, so they should be regularly removed. In any case, the quality of the foliage will eventually deteriorate, so it's best to sow in succession.

Dicentra spectabilis (Bleeding Heart)
A hardy perennial with superb foliage and attractive hanging flowers of red in a white cup. There is also an all-white variety. Both flower in early spring inside.

These perennials can be raised from seed sown in gentle heat in spring, but they'll take a year to reach flowering size. Alternatively lift a root from the garden in October or buy a plant from the garden centre. Pot them into 3½–4in. (9–10cm.) pots and put them in a semi-shaded position.

Feed with half-strength high potash fertiliser every fortnight, increasing to full strength when the plants are in flower. Water when the top of the compost is just moist.

After flowering, retain the plant for its foliage or replant in the garden.

Erica (Heather)
Heathers are hardy shrubs that prefer quite cold conditions so the majority should be brought into the house only for a short while when they are in flower. The one exception is *Erica gracilis*, which requires frost protection, but since it is prone to mildew it is best put in a cold frame after flowering.

They can be raised from cuttings taken in June or be bought from the garden centre. Pot them into 3½–4in. (9–10cm.) pots in a lime-free compost and put them in the sun out of draughts. Water when the top of the compost feels dry, using either rainwater or a solution of cold tea. Feed fortnightly with the high potash feed.

As soon as they have finished flowering, lightly trim them over, avoiding cutting back into the old wood, and put them outside.

Euonymus (Spindle Tree)
A hardy shrub with variegated foliage in shades of cream and green or silver and green.

It can be propagated by softwood cuttings in June or be bought from the garden centre. Pot into 4in. (10cm.) pots and put the plants in a sunny spot. Without light, the variegation tends to decrease. Water when the top of the compost feels just moist and feed fortnightly with the general-purpose feed.

In the spring, it pays to cut them back quite drastically to keep them compact. From the end of April until September, leave them outdoors.

Fatsia japonica (Japanese Aralia)
A more-or-less hardy shrub with superb, exotic foliage that will succumb outside only in the hardest frosts so should survive everywhere inside.

It can be raised from softwood cuttings in June or be air layered. Alternatively buy one from the shrub section of most garden centres.

Pot into a large pot or tub and set in a shady spot out of draughts. During the summer, feed once a week with the general-purpose feed and water when the top of the compost feels just moist. Keep the leaves clean by regular sponging. The variegated varieties are slightly more tender and demanding.

French Marigold
A cheap and cheerful houseplant if there ever was one. It will flower for a very long period from about May onwards but, since it's an annual, it should be discarded when it looks tatty. Recommended varieties are 'Little Nell' and 'Suzy Wong'.

Raise it in gentle heat from seed sown in February or March or buy it as a bedding plant from the garden centre. Pot into a 3in. (7.5cm.) pot and put it in full light. Water when the top of the compost feels dry and feed with high potash once a fortnight.

Fuchsia magellanica
A half-hardy shrub that needs cold conditions during summer but must be kept frost free in winter.

Propagate by softwood cuttings taken in early spring or in August. Pot young plants into 3–4in. (7.5–10cm.) pots and keep them in full light. Older plants will need larger pots but keep them as small as possible to encourage flowering. Pinch back young plants to encourage them to bush out, but it will take six weeks after pinching back for that shoot to flower again, so stop in April at the latest. Water when the top of the compost feels dry and feed fortnightly with the high potash fertiliser.

In the winter, keep the plants fairly dry and cool to rest them. Prune back drastically in early spring, repot if necessary and start watering a little more to encourage new growth.

French marigold
'Naughty Marietta'

Geranium

The common geranium makes a wonderful pot plant that will flower for ages and will put up with all sorts of maltreatment. It can be grown during the spring and summer in a cold room but it's also adaptable enough to be grown in cool conditions too.

It can be raised from softwood cuttings taken in August, but then it'll have to be kept over the winter and that's not easy. Much better raise geraniums from seed sown in gentle heat in January. They'll flower in June. Pot them into 4in. (10cm.) pots and give them full light. Water when the top of the compost feels dry and feed once a fortnight with the high potash feed.

After flowering, they can be cut back a bit and kept over the winter. If you decide to do this, keep them just frost free and very dry.

Left: Geranium 'Genie'

Above: *Dicentra spectabilis* 'Alba'

Below: *Fatsia japonica*

Hydrangea macrophylla

The large, mop-headed flowers make this a striking plant for cold rooms or the hallway. They are hardy shrubs that will grow to at least 3ft (0.9m.).

Propagate by softwood cuttings in June, but bear in mind that it will take about two years to reach flowering size. Plants are generally bought in flower in the spring. Put them in semi shade and water them when the top of the compost is dry. They appreciate an overhead spray as often as possible.

After they have finished flowering, put them outside. In June, prune back shoots that have flowered to leave about two buds of the current season's growth. Continue to water and feed with the high potash fertiliser once a fortnight. In the winter, put them in a frost-free place and keep them dry until February when they can be started into growth again.

Petunia

Another cheap and cheerful annual that gives tremendous value throughout the summer. Again, in less than ideal conditions, the plants are likely to deteriorate, so it's best to maintain a succession by sowing at intervals.

Choose an F_1 hybrid variety and sow in gentle heat from January onwards. Transplant to $3-3\frac{1}{2}$in. (7.5–9cm.) pots and put them in full light. Water when the compost feels dry and feed fortnightly with half-strength high potash feed. After flowering, the plants are discarded.

Primula

There are many primulas normally grown outside that will make excellent, cheap houseplants, and, given a cool room, they will flower for a long time. The alpine sink should not be without a few alpine primulas such as *P. auricula*, while some of the hardy garden varieties such as the common polyanthus, the primrose and cowslip can be lifted in October and potted for early spring flowering.

Several new strains of primrose are now being offered as seed and plants, and these will give their display of bright flowers in many colours for a long period. To raise them from seed choose a variety such as 'Saga' or 'Dolly Mixture' and sow from January to March in gentle heat. Pot into 3in. (7.5cm.) pots and put them a light spot out of direct sunlight. Water when the top of the compost feels just moist and feed with the high potash feed at half strength at fortnightly intervals.

After flowering, plant out in the garden or put them outside for the summer. Repot and divide if necessary in October and bring them back inside.

Roses

Miniature roses will give a good display of flowers in a cold room, but they should only be brought in for the flowering period. Afterwards they are best grown in the garden.

They can be propagated by cuttings in the autumn but they are better budded onto a special rootstock, so the best bet is to buy plants from the garden centre. Pot them into 6–7in. (15–17.5 cm.) pots in March but leave them outside until April. Set in full light and water when the top of the compost feels dry. Feed with the high potash feed once a fortnight.

After flowering, put them outside and continue to water and feed until September, when they should be allowed to rest. In March, prune back to leave about five good branches, which should be cut back to leave no more than three buds.

Salvia

This annual makes a bright splash of red and looks particularly good displayed with other annuals such as petunias.

Sow from January to March in gentle heat and pot into 3in. (7.5 cm.) pots. Put them in full light and water when the compost feels dry. Feed with half-strength potash once a fortnight.

After flowering, the plants should be discarded.

Schizanthus (Poor Man's Orchid)

An excellent pot plant that can be easily and cheaply raised from seed. It's best to choose a dwarf variety such as 'Star Parade'.

Sow in March to May in gentle heat for flowering in summer and in August or September for spring flowering. But bear in mind that overwintered plants will need frost protection. Grow them in $3\frac{1}{2}$–4in. (9–10cm.) pots and put them in full light but out of the direct sun. Water when the top of the compost feels just moist and feed once a fortnight with half-strength high potash feed.

Discard the plants after flowering.

Miniature rose

Salvia splendens
'Royal Mounty'

Viola

Though hardy perennials, these are best grown as half-hardy annuals. A wonderful range of colours and 'faces' is now available and they make cheering pot plants.

Sow in December or January for early summer flowering and in July for spring flowering. The July sowing is best made outside since high temperatures inhibit germination.

Alternatively, plants growing in the garden can be lifted and potted in October or they can be bought as early spring bedding plants from the garden centre. Pot into 3 in. (7.5 cm.) pots and put them in full light. Water when the compost is just moist and start feeding in spring with half-strength high potash fertiliser.

Remove flowers as they fade to encourage more. After flowering, the plants should be discarded.

Hydrangea hortensis

PLANTS FOR COOL ROOMS

The plants in this section constitute by far the largest group. Most houses these days will maintain at least the necessary 7°C (45°F) in the winter, even at night, and most of these plants will tolerate a rise to 18°C (65°F) during the day in the summer.

But do remember that it's these maximum and minimum temperatures that are important rather than the average daily temperature, so try to ensure that your plants never become subjected to colder or hotter conditions. In the winter, don't draw the curtains between a plant on the windowsill and the room. Bring it into the middle of the room at night where it will be warmer. In the summer, if you expect the temperature to rise above the maximum recommended, move the plants permanently to a shadier, cooler spot. Try not to move them when they are in flower, however, or they may drop their buds.

Many plants in this group will thrive outdoors during the summer. In most parts of the country it would be safe to put them outside after the first week in June and bring them back inside after the last week in September. Naturally, if a frost is forecast the plants must be brought back into the house straight away.

When they are outside, plunge them into a bed of peat or sand or into the garden soil. This will keep the roots a little cooler and moister and reduce the amount of watering necessary. And, quite important, it will also ensure that they don't fall over. Don't forget them when they're outside. They will still need watering and feeding at regular intervals.

Aloe variegata (Partridge-Breasted Aloe)
This succulent plant is grown mainly for its spiky leaves, which are green striped white. It produces a bonus in early spring of an orange-red flower spike.

It can be raised from seed sown in spring in warmth, about 21°C (70°F), but germination is slow and erratic. Don't give up for at least six months. The plants will also produce offsets, and these can be removed when they have a few roots and potted into 3in. (7.5cm.) pots.

Put them in good light but out of direct sun. Water when the top of the compost feels just moist and feed with the general fertiliser once a month in the summer. Never allow water or fertiliser to rest between the scaly leaves, since this may rot them.

Aralia elegantissima
The posh name for this easy foliage plant is *Dizygotheca*, but I doubt if you'll ever find it sold as that.

It's easy to raise from seed sown in spring in warmth, 21–24°C (70–75 °F). Put the sown pot into a polythene bag in the airing cupboard to maintain humidity. They should germinate in three to four weeks.

Pot into 3in. (7.5cm.) pots and keep potting on as required. Put them in good light but out of direct sunlight and water when the top of the compost feels dry. During the growing season feed with the general fertiliser once a month. They like a high humidity so stand the pots on gravel in a saucer of water and spray regularly.

Araucaria heterophylla (Norfolk Island Pine)
A relative of the monkey puzzle tree (but not nearly so vicious), this tree will grow to about 5ft (1.5m.), but it's very slow growing so it makes a fine houseplant.

It's very difficult to propagate, though if you fancy your chances you may try raising it from seed. I've never managed it. Put it in good light but out of direct sun and water when the compost feels just moist. Feed with the general fertiliser every fortnight in the growing season, and spray overhead frequently.

In the summer it can go outside. A large specimen makes a fine patio plant but put it in a sheltered spot.

Asparagus Ferns
These are not ferns at all, but members of the lily family. Two that are very easy to grow from seed and make excellent foliage plants are *Asparagus plumosus nanus*, which has very finely divided fern-like foliage, and *A. sprengeri*, which has lax, semi-trailing fronds of small leaflets. They make very good hanging basket plants.

Sow the seeds in a temperature of 16–21°C (60–70°F) and they should germinate in about four weeks. Plant them in 3in. (7.5cm.) pots and pot them on only when the roots are well out of the container. They like to be cramped but they must also have plenty of feed, so give them a weekly dose of the general fertiliser. Water when the compost feels just moist – they must never be allowed to dry out. They like good light out of direct sun and they can be put outside during the summer for a health cure.

If they get straggly, cut them back hard and feed them well. They'll soon put out new shoots.

Aspidistra elatior (Cast-Iron Plant)

A really tough character that will stand any amount of neglect. However, you'll have a much better plant if you care for it. Still it is not a bad one to start with if you're not used to growing plants.

These plants will always throw up offsets, which can be used for propagation. Simply cut through the rootball to separate them and pot them individually into small pots at first, potting on as needed. They like a semi-shaded position and should not be allowed to dry completely, so water when the compost feels just moist.

Keep the leaves clean by sponging regularly and feed in the spring and summer with the general-purpose feed, once a month. Aspidistras prefer to be slightly cramped so only repot them when the roots are pushing out of the container.

Araucaria heterophylla

Begonia

There are several types of begonias, needing somewhat different treatment. In this section, the fibrous-rooted *Begonia semperflorens* and the tuberous *B. tuberhybrida* are included because they will grow well in cool conditions. For foliage begonias see p. 112. Fibrous-rooted begonias are

Above: *Asparagus sprengeri*
Left: *Aloe variegata*
Centre: *Aspidistra elatior*
Right: *Aralia elegantissima*

grown as annuals, though they can be grown on for another year if high enough temperatures can be maintained in winter.

Sow in January or February in warmth, 21–24°C (70–75°F). The seed is very fine indeed, so it's best mixed with sand first, and left uncovered. Transfer the seedlings to 3–3½in. (7.5–9cm.) pots when they are big enough to handle and put them in good light but out of direct sunlight. Feed once a fortnight with the high potash fertiliser and water when the top of the compost feels just moist.

These plants can also be grown in the garden during the summer and, if you have done so, they can be lifted, cut back a little and potted as houseplants. They'll continue to flower until well into the New Year and could well go on for the following year.

Tuberous begonias are treated differently. These are best bought as tubers and started into growth in February by potting them into 5–6in. (12.5–15cm.) pots, making sure that the concave side of the tuber is uppermost. Put them in indirect sunlight and water when the top of the compost feels dry. Feed with high potash fertiliser every fortnight. Tuberous begonias appreciate high humidity, so stand the pots in a water-filled tray of gravel.

When flowering is over in the autumn, feeding should stop and watering be reduced until the foliage dies down. The tubers can then be stored until the following February. They will increase in size each year and can be cut into pieces, provided each piece has a visible bud.

Browallia speciosa
A beautiful, delicate-looking, flowering plant that is, in fact, as tough as old boots. It makes a superb hanging basket plant. It is easily raised from seed, which should be sown in early spring and late summer for flowering in about four to five months. It prefers a light place, but not direct sun, and it should not be allowed to dry out so water when the compost feels just moist. Overfeeding produces foliage at the expense of flowers, so feed with the high potash fertiliser every month.

Cacti
There are hundreds of different cacti, most of which will be quite happy in cool conditions. They all require much the same treatment. Most will flower but they'll need lots of light and you will need patience.

Most can be raised easily from seed sown at any time though, because of their requirement for plenty of light, the early spring is best in my opinion. Sow in warmth, 21–27°C (70–80°F), and don't allow the seedlings to dry out. Pot into small pots in a soil-based compost with extra grit and put in full sunlight. Water when the top of the compost feels dry and feed once a month with the general fertiliser in the spring and summer. In the winter, they should be kept quite dry.

Calceolaria (Slipper Flower)

These stunning half-hardy annuals are easy to grow and make excellent, cheap pot plants. Choose a variety like 'Anytime', which can be raised from seed sown at any time of the year in a temperature of 21–24°C (70–75°F).

Transfer the seedlings to 3–3½in. (7.5–9cm.) pots and put them in full but indirect sunlight. Feed fortnightly with the high potash fertiliser at half strength and water when the top of the compost feels just moist. Remove faded blooms and make sure you watch out for greenfly.

Capsicum (Ornamental Pepper)

These plants are grown for their ornamental fruits rather than their flowers, which are insignificant.

They are easily raised from seed sown in March in a temperature of 18–21°C (65–70°F). Transfer to 3–3½in. (7.5–9cm.) pots and put them in bright but indirect sunlight. Water when the compost feels just moist and feed with the high potash feed once every three weeks, until the fruits start to colour, and then at weekly intervals. Stand the pots on gravel over water and spray regularly. Watch out for greenfly, which are almost certain to attack.

Chamaedorea elegans (Parlour Palm)

Often sold as *Neanthe bella*, this small palm is easy to grow and will not become enormous. It can be raised from seed, but this is only for the expert. Stand the potted plant on a layer of gravel in a water-filled tray in a semi-shaded spot. If the atmosphere becomes too dry the tips of the leaves will turn brown. Water when the top of the compost feels just moist and feed fortnightly with the general fertiliser. Pot on when the roots completely fill the container.

Chlorophytum (Spider Plant)

We've all seen it, we've almost certainly all grown it – and what terrible tatty specimens most of them are.

However, they need not be if grown properly. The answer is to feed them copiously and the foliage will then become wider, more colourful and shinier.

Propagate by taking off the numerous plantlets it produces and rooting them in water. Transfer them to compost in $3\frac{1}{2}$in. (9cm.) pots when roots begin to form. Put them in a sunny spot but out of direct sunlight and water when the top of the compost feels dry. Feed at every watering in the spring and summer, using general fertiliser.

It will probably be necessary to repot every year in the spring, so when plants start to get too big for your biggest pot make sure you have a replacement plant coming on.

Above: *Chlorophytum*

Below: *Chamaedorea elegans*
(*Neanthe bella*)

Right: *Capsicum annuum*

Chrysanthemum

One of the most popular of flowering plants, these can be bought in flower at any time of the year. When you do buy one, make sure the plant is well shaped and that the flower buds are just opening.

Though it's easy enough to root cuttings, houseplant chrysanthemums should not be propagated since the new plants would finish up several feet tall with few flowers, unless treated with growth-retarding chemicals, as is done commercially.

Keep them in a sunny spot out of direct sunlight and water moderately – only when the top of the compost is quite dry. Feeding and repotting are not necessary.

After flowering, the plants should be discarded. They will not survive in the garden and, though they could be cut down and grown again, they would not be worth the effort.

Chrysanthemum
'Orange Wonder'

Cineraria

This popular flowering plant is sometimes listed under its Latin name *Senecio cruentus*. It comes in a wide range of superb colours and is very floriferous.

Raise it from seed sown from April to August in a temperature of about 18–21°C (65–70°F). It will flower in about six months from sowing, so it's possible to stagger the sowings for a succession of flowers. Put it in indirect sunlight and out of draughts and water it copiously when the top of the compost feels moist. This is one plant that really drinks it up, so it's best to soak it in the sink. Feed every three weeks with half-strength high potash fertiliser.

This is another certain candidate for greenfly, and whitefly like it too, so watch out. After flowering, the plants are discarded.

Cissus antarctica (Kangaroo Vine)
Rhoicissus capensis (Grape Ivy)

These two are described together because there is very little difference between the plants and none between their treatment. Both are climbing or trailing foliage plants. They will twine round any support or they can be used in hanging baskets as a trailer.

Both can be propagated by tip cuttings taken in spring or summer or by layering. Put the plants in indirect sunlight and water when the top of the compost feels just moist. Feed every two weeks with the general fertiliser.

They will probably need repotting every spring and, when the container size is big enough, remove the top few inches of compost and replace with fresh. Keep the leaves clean and free from dust and, in the early stages of the plant's life particularly, pinch out the growing tips regularly to encourage bushy growth.

Citrus (Orange Tree)

The citrus family includes all orange and lemon species. They can all be raised quite easily from pips taken from fruit you have eaten (see p.24), but the varieties you buy in the florist or garden centre will probably have been grafted and are more likely to fruit. If you do buy one, make sure it has some fruit on it. Put the plants in a well-lit place out of direct sunlight and, in the spring and summer, water when the compost feels dry on the top. Feed weekly during the summer with the high potash fertiliser.

In the winter, put the plant in a cold but frost-free room and water it very little. Don't feed at all. Then, in the spring, bring it into more heat, repot if necessary and start to increase the watering. This is also the time to prune, but this should be done only if it's really necessary to shape the plant.

Cycas revoluta (Sago Palm)

A feathery fronded palm that makes a superb feature in the room. It's very slow growing unfortunately and difficult to propagate from seed.

Put it in a well-lit spot out of direct sun and water when the top of the compost feels dry. Feed every fortnight in summer with the general fertiliser.

In the winter it needs little water and will tolerate lower temperatures – though they should never drop below $13°C$ ($55°F$).

Cyclamen persicum

One of the most popular flowering plants at Christmas, and thousands must be given as presents. Unfortunately, thousands die fairly rapidly because they are put in the centrally heated lounge where they can be admired. The ideal temperature is about $10°C$ ($50°F$) so, if you want to keep one, put it in a colder room. If the buds start to drop and the leaves go yellow, it is probably because the plant is too hot.

Cyclamen can easily be raised from seed sown from August to March. Those sown in August will flower at Christmas the following year. Soak the seed before sowing in pots or boxes and cover with a layer of sharp sand. They need a temperature of $16-18°C$ ($60-65°F$), higher temperatures inhibiting germination. Transfer the seedlings into 3in. (7.5cm.) pots and, as they grow, repot until they are finally in a $6\frac{1}{2}$in. (16.5cm.) pot for the largest plants. Put them in bright, but not direct, sunlight and water when the top of the compost feels quite dry. They require little feeding so use a half-strength high potash feed at fortnightly intervals until flower buds show and then increase it to full strength.

After flowering, the leaves will begin to turn yellow and then water should be withdrawn gradually. Leave the plant unwatered for two months and then remove the corm, clean it up and repot it, with the top just above the surface.

Cymbidium

If you think that orchids are way out of reach, think again. This one is pretty easy to grow and produces the most exotic of all flowers. It is well worth the trouble. The variety 'Peter Pan' is probably the best one to buy.

Having bought a plant, they can be propagated by taking off the little bulbs (pseudobulbs) that form around the base of the plant. Take a bit of root with them and pot them up into the special compost suggested on p. 32. They want indirect sunlight and a humid atmosphere, so stand them in gravel-filled water trays, and spray overhead with water. Water very infrequently, only when the top of the compost is bone dry, and don't feed at all. Repot in the special orchid compost when roots start to appear on the surface.

Above left: *Citrus mitis*

Below left: *Cissus antarctica*

Above: *Cineraria (Senecio)*

Cyclamen persicum

Epiphyllum (Orchid Cactus)
Rhipsalidopsis gaertneri (Easter Cactus)
These cacti have flattened stems that can grow a couple of feet long. Both bear large red blooms in the spring so they make quite a dramatic basket plant.

They are not difficult to propagate. Take tip cuttings 4–5in. (10–12.5cm.) long, allow them to dry for a couple of days and then put them in a pot of compost. They need no heat. Put them in a well-lit spot and water when the top of the compost feels just moist. When the plants bud up, water more copiously and feed them with half-strength high potash fertiliser once a fortnight. Don't move the plant when it has buds on or they'll drop. In the winter, move them to a cool room and keep them on the dry side.

Fatshedera lizei (Ivy Tree)
An evergreen semi-climber with ivy-like leaves. It will grow to about 4ft (1.2m.), making an attractive feature plant. There is also a variegated form.

The best way to propagate it is from stem cuttings taken in the summer. Pot them into $3\frac{1}{2}$–4in. (9–10cm.) pots and put them in a shady spot. (The variegated form needs slightly more light.) Water when the top of the compost feels just moist and feed with the general fertiliser fortnightly. Pot the plants on as the roots fill the pot, and provide some support for the stems. Pinching back regularly will encourage bushier growth.

In the winter, stop feeding and water when the top of the compost feels dry.

Gerbera (Transvaal Daisy)
The stunning clarity of the colours of gerberas makes them a talking point wherever they're seen. New dwarf varieties, which are easy to grow, will make this one of the most popular new introductions, I'm sure.

Raise them from seed, choosing a variety such as 'Happi-pot', which will grow 8–12in. (20–30cm.) tall. Sow in spring and summer in a temperature of about 18–21°C (65–70°F) and keep the trays in light, which is needed for germination. Pot them into $3\frac{1}{2}$in. (9cm.) pots and pot on as necessary to flowering size, which is about a 6in. (15cm.) pot.

Put them in a sunny spot out of direct sunlight and water when the top of the compost feels just moist. Feed in the summer with the high potash feed every two weeks.

Hedera helix (Ivy)

Ivies are tough plants, but that shouldn't mean that they can be treated roughly. They'll make much better plants if you love them a little. There are many varieties with different leaf shapes and colours, many of them variegated.

Cuttings will root quite easily in June and they should be potted up into small pots and potted on progressively. Put the green-leaved types in a shady spot and those with variegated leaves in rather more light to ensure that they keep their colour. Pinch back regularly to maintain a bushy habit and, if they do become leggy, cut them back hard and start again. Water when the top of the compost feels dry, and feed in the growing season with the general fertiliser.

Hippeastrum

Often wrongly called amaryllis, this popular Christmas present produces huge, trumpet-shaped flowers in a variety of colours.

Pot the bulb into a pot of a size appropriate to the size of the bulb. They like to be potbound, so don't choose too large a container. They will flower in the winter or spring, and the flower will be followed by leaves. To build up the flower for next year, it's important to grow them well from now on. Water when the top of the compost feels just moist and feed with the potash fertiliser every two weeks. A spell outside would do them a power of good but only after all danger of frosts has passed.

As soon as the leaves show signs of withering, gradually withdraw water and stop feeding. This will happen in early autumn. Leave the bulb in the room in a light place where it will rest for a while. As soon as you see the first sign of regrowth, carefully scrape a little compost from the top of the pot, refill and start watering again.

Impatiens (Busy Lizzie)

This is another plant that has been much improved by the breeders. It's easily raised from seed, is available in a variety of colours and makes an excellent pot and hanging basket plant.

Sow in gentle heat in March, choosing an F_1 hybrid. Pot the plants into $3-3\frac{1}{2}$in. (7.5–9cm.) pots and put them in the lightest spot you've got away from direct sun.

Above: *Hippeastrum*
Right: *Fatshedera lizei* 'Pia'

Water when the top of the compost feels just moist and feed with the high potash fertiliser once a month.

They can be grown on for another year since they are perennial, but you'll have better results from sowing new seed each year. If you have plants growing in the garden, they can be potted in the autumn, cut back a little and used as pot plants in the same way as fibrous begonias.

Left: *Gerbera*
Below: *Impatiens*

Jasminum polyanthum (Jasmine)

This winter-flowering climber has a superb fragrance and is a must for the cool room.

It can easily be propagated by stem cuttings in June. Pot them into 4in. (10cm.) pots and pinch out the tips when they are 12in. (30cm.) tall. The wiry shoots will need support so either grow them up a framework or make a circle of wire, which should be stuck into the pot so that the shoots can be trained in circular fashion around it.

Put in a sunny spot and water when the top of the compost feels just moist. Feed with the high potash fertiliser once a fortnight in the summer. When the plants have finished flowering, pluck up all your courage and cut them down to within 6in. (15cm.) of the pot.

Myrtus communis (Myrtle)

An evergreen shrub with fragrant flowers and aromatic foliage. It can be propagated by stem cuttings in June, but take plenty, for not all will root.

Put the plants in a sunny spot and make sure that the pots are turned regularly, so that they grow evenly. Any branches that spoil the shape can be pruned lightly. Water with rainwater or cold tea when the top of the compost is just moist and feed with the high potash feed every fortnight. Stop feeding in the autumn and reduce watering but keep the plant in a sunny spot. Repot in the spring when growth recommences.

Nertera granadensis (Bead Plant)

A low-growing creeper that will form a small, berry-covered mound. Grow it in a large plastic saucer used normally to catch water under pots, but drill a couple of drainage holes in the bottom.

Plants can be raised from seed sown in the spring in a temperature of 18–21°C (65–70°F). Pot up the seedlings into the trays and put them in a sunny spot. Water when the top of the compost feels just moist and feed only when the plant appears to have stopped growing. Too much fertiliser and they will make lots of foliage at the expense of flowers and berries. Use the high potash feed at half strength in the growing season.

Passiflora caerulea (Passion Flower)

A passion flower is hard to beat as a conversation stopper. The flowers are so symmetrical and perfectly formed that they can't fail to catch the eye. This is another climber that does well trained around a wire support.

It can easily be propagated from stem cuttings in June or by layering. Put it in a sunny spot and give it a spell outside in the summer if you can. Water when the top of the compost feels just moist and, in the summer, feed fortnightly with the high potash feed.

After flowering, cut back the stems to 6in. (15cm.). It needs infrequent repotting since it will flower better if potbound.

Pilea (Aluminium Plant)
A small evergreen with green leaves beautifully marked with silver.

It is easily propagated by stem cuttings in June. Pot into 3in. (7.5cm.) pots and put in bright but indirect sunlight. In a dark spot these plants may lose their colouring. Water when the top of the compost feels just moist and feed fortnightly in summer with the general fertiliser. Keep pinching back the shoot tips to maintain a bushy habit.

Rhipsalidopsis gaertneri (Easter Cactus)
see *Epiphyllum (Orchid Cactus)*

Rhododendron simsii (Indian Azalea) (syn. Azalea indica)
A popular Christmas present and an unpopular disaster in more cases than is necessary. They are not at all difficult to grow provided they are given the right conditions.

Protect the plant from cold on the way home by putting it in a polythene bag – even if you're in the car. Never, never buy this or any other half-hardy plant from an outside display. When you get the plant home, put it in the coolest room you've got above freezing, and spray it with water. Continue spraying regularly: it's high temperatures and low humidity that cause the buds to drop.

Put it in a bright spot but out of direct sunlight and water frequently. It should never be allowed to dry out for a moment so keep an eye on it and water when the compost still feels fairly moist, using rainwater or cold tea. As the flowers fade, carefully take them off and, in the summer, put the plant outside. It still needs to be watered regularly and should be fed fortnightly with the high potash fertiliser. In September bring it indoors and it should flower again, though probably a little later than the previous season.

Above: *Jasminum polyanthum*

Below: *Saxifraga stolonifera sarmentosa*

Right: *Nertera*

Opposite: *Passiflora*

The plants can be propagated by stem cuttings in June but they are not easy so take plenty.

The Indian azalea is not hardy so it can't be planted in the garden, but some florists and garden centres are now offering hardy azaleas as pot plants flowering in spring. They are fine as houseplants and can be planted out afterwards. Treat them in the same way as the Indian azalea.

Rhoicissus capensis
see *Cissus antarctica*

Saxifraga stolonifera (Mother of Thousands)
Easy to grow, easy to propagate and attractive but perhaps unfairly shunned as being too common. It's an interesting plant that produces dozens of small plantlets on long runners, making it a good plant for hanging baskets. The runners can simply be detached and planted in pots, where they'll root easily. Put it in good but indirect sunlight and water when the top of the compost feels just moist. Feed once a fortnight in summer with the high potash fertiliser. The plant bears clusters of flowers that are attractive but after flowering it dies, so make sure you have taken plantlets as replacements.

Schlumbergera (Christmas Cactus) (syn. Zygocactus)

This flat-stemmed cactus, which has pink/red flowers just before Christmas, is easily propagated by removing a section of stem, leaving it to dry for a few days and then potting up. Put it in bright but indirect sunlight and feed every three weeks with half-strength high potash fertiliser in the summer.

While the plants are growing, water them when the top of the compost feels just moist, but in the autumn they should be given a rest so water less frequently. Put them in a bright but cold position, 13°C (55°F), preferably in the spare room. They will produce more flower buds if they are in a dark room at night. When the buds begin to appear, move the plants into a slightly warmer room in good sunlight.

Solanum capsicastrum (Winter Cherry)

Easy to grow and cheap to buy, these produce brightly coloured berries in the winter just when they're needed.

They are easily raised from seed sown in February or March in gentle heat, 18°C (65°F). Pot the seedlings into 3½in. (9cm.) pots and stand them outside throughout the summer. When the flowers appear, they should be sprayed with water daily to assist pollination. Feed them every fortnight with the high potash feed. Bring them inside in October and put in a bright place, watering when the top of the compost feels dry. After the berries fall, cut the plant back to about a third and begin again.

Streptocarpus (Cape Primrose)

Excellent plants to grow from seed. The wide, trumpet-shaped flowers come in an extensive variety of colours, from white through red to purple.

Choose an F$_1$ hybrid and sow in gentle heat, 21°C (70°F), in February or March. Pot the plants into 3½–4in. (9–10cm.) pots and put in a slightly shaded position. Water when the top of the compost feels just moist and feed with the high potash fertiliser once a fortnight.

In the winter, the plants should be rested by leaving them in a cool but frost-free room and watering sparingly.

If you raise a good coloured plant from seed and wish to propagate it, you can do so by taking leaf cuttings. In the summer, cut a leaf along the mid-rib and set the two cut halves in compost. Provide a little gentle bottom heat and a row of plantlets will form along the cut edge.

Thunbergia (Black-eyed Susan)

A superb annual climber that makes an excellent hanging basket plant, trailing to about 4ft (1.2m.) and studded with orange flowers with black centres.

Sow in March or April in gentle heat, 18°C (65°F). Pot into 3½in. (9cm.) pots, put in a sunny position and water when the top of the compost feels just moist. Feed fortnightly with high potash fertiliser. After the flowering, it is possible to cut the plant back and start again. However, it may not flower so well the second year so it's best to re-sow.

Tolmiea (Piggyback Plant)

An unusual foliage plant that carries a small plantlet on each leaf. If the leaves are removed with a well-developed plantlet, they can be potted up to make another plant.

Put in a sunny spot but out of direct sunlight and water when the top of the compost feels just moist. Feed fortnightly with the general fertiliser. In the winter reduce the water and stop feeding.

Tradescantia (Wandering Jew)

An attractive trailing plant that is extremely easy to propagate. If you can't root stem cuttings from this one, give up and take up arc welding! There are several different colours to choose from, varying from deep red/brown to variegated silver and green.

The trouble with the plant is that, as it grows older and longer, the bottom leaves fall off and it looks rather ugly at the base. Delay this problem by pinching out regularly and, when a shoot looks ugly, cut it out completely and replace with a cutting.

The cuttings can be rooted in water in a matter of days and potted into individual pots. Put them in a bright spot out of direct sunlight and water when the top of the compost feels just moist. Feed fortnightly with the general fertiliser. Reduce watering in the winter and stop feeding. If variegated shoots revert to green, cut them out.

Vinca (Periwinkle)

An attractive little annual easily raised from seed.

Sow in March in gentle heat, 18°C (65°F), and pot into 3½in. (9cm.) pots. Put the plants in a brightly lit spot out of direct sunlight and water when the top of the compost feels just moist. Feed fortnightly with the high potash feed. After flowering discard the plants.

Above: *Tolmiea*
Below: *Yucca elephantipes*
Right: *Solanum capsicastrum*

Above: *Streptocarpus*

Left: *Thunbergia*

Yucca (Spanish Bayonet)

Striking foliage plants that will make fine specimens on their own or as the centrepiece of a group. Some yuccas (for example, *Y. aloifolia*) will grow a trunk with the spikes of foliage on top. They will keep growing taller and taller and may eventually outgrow the room. A recent trend is for nurserymen to grow *Y. elephantipes*, which they propagate from stems imported from the Caribbean. The stems are rooted and then grow a head of foliage on top. They will not increase in height so at least you know what you've got, and you can buy them in different sizes.

Y. aloifolia can be propagated from seed but germination is slow, often up to twelve months, and erratic. Put the plants in the lightest place in the room and, if you can give them a summer holiday outside, so much the better. In the growing season, feed with the general fertiliser every fortnight and water well when the compost feels just moist.

In the winter bring them indoors and rest them by reducing the water and stopping feeding.

PLANTS FOR WARM ROOMS

Certainly the most difficult spot in the house for plants is the centrally heated living room. And that, of course, is where we most want them. The plants must therefore be carefully chosen and the conditions must be tailored to suit them as much as possible.

Unfortunately there are two big problems: plants that like high temperatures generally like high humidity too; and they like their surroundings to be hot *all* the time, not just during the day. So, a centrally heated house is not the ideal environment.

Nonetheless, we can go some way towards meeting their needs. With careful choice, there's no reason at all why the living room should not house a fine collection. Those in this section require a temperature of 16–24°C (60–75°F) and should never fall below 13°C (55°F) even for a short time. So in the winter, it's extremely important not to isolate plants on the windowsill by drawing the curtains.

Achimenes (Hot-Water Plant)
A compact, dome-shaped plant that is covered in flowers for a very long period. There are several varieties to choose from in a range of reds, blues and white.

The best way to start is to buy the small tubercles which are obtainable from most seedsmen. Pot them up in the spring and give them a temperature of about 18°C (65°F). When shoots appear, they can be put in slightly cooler conditions. They like a sunny spot out of direct sunlight, and the compost must never be allowed to dry out. Water when the top feels moist to the touch. Feed at fortnightly intervals with the high potash fertiliser.

Flowering will finish in the early autumn and, then, water should gradually be withdrawn and feeding should stop. When the foliage has died down, store the tubercles dry either in the pot or in dry sand, and restart them the following year.

Anthurium (Flamingo Flower)
Brilliant red spathes and shiny green foliage make this a desirable if somewhat difficult plant.

Propagation is very difficult, involving a lot of heat and

a long wait for seed to germinate, but, once you have a plant, it can be divided in spring.

They like the higher end of the temperature scale and should be stood on gravel in a water-filled tray to provide humidity. Put them in bright light, but out of direct sun, and water when the top of the compost feels just moist, using rainwater or cold tea. Feed with the high potash fertiliser at half strength every fortnight. In the winter, they can stand lower temperatures and drier compost.

Aphelandra (Zebra Plant)
Distinctly variegated leaves and a bright yellow spike of bracts make this a striking specimen.

Achimenes

Left: *Aphelandra squarrosa*
Above: *Anthurium andreanum*

They can be propagated by stem cuttings in June. Put them in indirect light and keep humid by regular spraying and by placing the plant over water standing on gravel.

Water when the top of the compost feels just moist but bear in mind that the leaves naturally droop so don't make the mistake of over-watering because they appear to be wilting. Feed with the high potash fertiliser at fortnightly intervals.

In the winter, give the plant a rest by putting it in a slightly cooler spot and watering when the top of the compost feels dry. Don't feed at all. After flowering, the bracts will turn green and can then be cut off to encourage further growth.

Begonia rex

Apart from this variety, there are several other superb foliage begonias, all of which can be treated in the same way.

They can be propagated quite successfully by leaf cuttings or by seed, the latter taking longer to produce a large plant. Put them in a light place out of direct sunlight to ensure that they retain their colours, and water when the top of the compost feels just moist. Feed with the general fertiliser every fortnight in the summer.

In the winter, rest them by giving less water and no feed.

Beloperone guttata (Shrimp Plant)

I have had shrimp plants that have not stopped flowering all year, so they certainly earn their keep. The 'flowers' are actually bracts from which white flowers appear in the late spring.

They can be increased by taking stem cuttings in June. Put them in a sunny window and water when the top of the compost feels just moist. Feed every fortnight in the summer with the high potash fertiliser.

In the spring, prune them back to leave about 6in. (15cm.). Rest the plant in the winter by reducing water, omitting feed and lowering temperatures.

Bromeliads

These exotic plants include the urn plant (*Aechmea*), the pineapple (*Ananas*) and the scarlet star (*Guzmania*). They all produce striking flower spikes from the centre of each plant but, when the flower dies, so do the plants. They do, however, leave behind a number of smaller offsets at the base of the mother plant, and these can be potted up to start again.

Allow the offsets to become well established and then cut them away. Pot them into a lime-free compost and put them in a sunny window. Water when the top of the compost feels just moist and keep the 'urn' in the centre of the plant filled up. Feed monthly with the high potash fertiliser.

During the winter stop feeding and water less, keeping the urn dry.

Caladium hybrids (Angel's Wings)
Surely the most delicate of foliage plants, these tuberous-rooted arums come in a wide range of colours, from green and white to red on green. They aren't easy to grow but are worth a little extra trouble.

They can be propagated by division in the spring, removing the offsets and repotting.

The tubers are started into growth in the spring after storage through the winter. Remove the plant from its pot and break away the old soil. Repot into fresh compost and put in good but indirect sunlight.

In the summer, water when the compost feels just moist so as to avoid drying out, and feed fortnightly with the general fertiliser. Provide humidity by standing the pot over a tray of water and by spraying regularly.

The leaves will begin to die down in the autumn and that's a sign that it's time for a rest. Gradually stop watering and feeding and, when the leaves have died right down, cut them off and store the pot at not less than 16°C (60°F), watering very, very little.

Calathea (Peacock Plant)
A delicate foliage plant whose leaves look as though they have been painted by a Japanese artist. There are several interesting and beautiful colour combinations. It's a difficult plant to grow because it likes high temperatures and, even more important, high humidity, which must be provided by standing the pot on gravel in a water tray.

It can be divided when it is repotted but it's probably better to keep the well-shaped plant. Put it in semi-shade and water when the top of the compost feels just moist. Feed with the general fertiliser every fortnight. During the winter, keep the same watering and temperature regime, but don't feed.

Codiaeum (Croton)
A striking foliage plant available in many shades of red, pink, yellow and orange.

It can be propagated by taking stem cuttings in June or it can be air layered, like a rubber plant.

It needs the sunniest place in the room and, like most of the heat lovers, a humid atmosphere. Water when the top

Above: *Beloperone*

Below: *Caladium*

Above right: *Guzmania* 'Claudine'

Below right: *Calathea crocata*

of the compost feels just moist and feed fortnightly with the general fertiliser. Maintain the same temperature and watering regime in the winter, but cut out the fertiliser.

Codiaeum variegatum 'Mrs Iceton'

Columnea (Goldfish Vine)

Again, not an easy plant to grow but one that is well worth trying. It looks extremely attractive in a hanging basket, where it will trail downwards several feet. The growths are covered with a fine down of red or purple and the red and yellow tubular flowers are borne in profusion.

It responds quite well to propagation by tip cuttings, which should be taken after flowering has finished.

Put the plants in bright but indirect sunlight and maintain humidity by regular spraying. Water when the top of the compost feels just moist and feed with the high potash fertiliser every two weeks. In the winter, rest the plants by cutting down watering and stopping feeding.

Dieffenbachia (Dumb Cane)
This fine foliage plant is definitely not for a family with inquisitive young children. If a child puts a bit of leaf into his mouth, it will cause very painful swellings – hence the common name. But provided you don't eat the darned thing, it makes a fine foliage plant.

It can easily be propagated from stem cuttings, which will root readily in water. Pot them up and put in a light position but out of direct sunlight. Water when the top of the compost feels just moist and, in the summer, feed fortnightly with the general fertiliser. Maintain humidity by placing the plant in a tray of water with the pot standing on gravel and by spraying regularly.

If the plant deteriorates, it can be cut back to about 4in. (10cm.) and the stem used to make more plants. In the winter, maintain similar temperatures and watering but stop feeding.

Dracaena terminalis (syn. Cordyline terminalis)
Brilliantly coloured foliage that will set off a collection of green foliage plants to perfection.

Propagate by removing offsets when repotting in the spring. Put the plants in indirect sunlight and water when the top of the compost feels just moist. Feed with the general fertiliser once a fortnight in the summer.

In the winter, maintain the same temperatures but reduce watering and stop feeding.

Euphorbia (Poinsettia)
The brilliant red bracts of the poinsettia are as much a reminder of Christmas as 'Good King Wenceslas', but because it's sold at a cold time of the year, great care must be taken when taking it home. Like the azaleas, it should not be bought from an outside display and it should be protected by a polythene bag on the journey. Treated well, it will continue to give a fine display until well into spring and often longer.

It can be propagated from stem cuttings but, since the plants you buy are treated with a dwarfing chemical, expect a very much bigger plant. It's also very tricky getting the bracts to colour up again so it's really hardly worth it.

Water when the top of the compost feels just moist and feed every two weeks in the summer with the high potash fertiliser.

If you feel you must try to get the plant to produce another show next Christmas, cut it back after the bracts have fallen and put it outside after early June. Bring it inside in October and for eight weeks give it no more than ten hours of light and fourteen hours of darkness. To do this put a black polythene bag over its head or place it in a cupboard. Then bring it back into normal light. In the winter, keep watering but stop feeding.

Exacum affine

A compact flowering plant with masses of fragrant blue flowers with golden centres. Easily raised from seed sown in February for a late summer/autumn flowering and in September to flower in spring. Sow in a temperature of 18–21°C (65–70°F) and transfer to $3\frac{1}{2}$–4in. (9–10cm.) pots when the seedlings are large enough.

Put them in indirect sunlight in the cooler part of the room – but out of draughts – and water when the top of the compost feels just moist. Feed once a fortnight with the high potash feed. After flowering the plants are discarded.

Ferns

There are several different types of fern but most like similar conditions so I have put them together.

Those such as the bird's nest fern (Asplenium) and the ribbon brake fern (Pteris) require high temperatures whereas the Boston fern (Nephrolepis) and the maidenhair fern (Adiantum) will be happy in low ones. All need a bright spot but out of direct sunlight and, in fact, they'll tolerate a bit of shade. It's important to provide humidity by standing the pots on gravel in a water-filled tray.

Many can be propagated by seed (spores) which can be obtained from some seedsmen. Keep them fairly damp by watering when the top of the compost feels moist and feed monthly with the general fertiliser. In the winter, stop feeding and reduce water a little.

Below: *Dieffenbachia*

Right: *Columnea microphylla* 'Stavanger'

Ficus (Rubber Plant. Fig)

Still the most popular of all foliage plants, the rubber plant (*F. robusta*) is king. However, it's closely followed by its cousin the weeping fig (*F. benjamina*), while the creeping fig (*F. pumila*) is also gaining in popularity.

The two figs are easy to propagate from stem cuttings in June, and the rubber plant can be air layered if it gets too tall or loses its bottom leaves.

The leaves are large and will pick up dust easily, clogging the pores, so sponge them regularly.

Put all but the creeping fig in indirect sunlight. The creeper will do quite well in semi shade. Be careful not to overwater, watering only when the top of the compost feels dry. In the summer, feed with the general fertiliser once a fortnight. In the winter, rest the plants by reducing watering and stopping feeding.

Left: *Ficus benjamina*
Above: *Ficus robusta*

Pot on in the spring but only when the roots fill the pot since they like being a bit cramped.

Gloxinia
This plant is sometimes listed under its Latin name, *Sinningia speciosa*, so don't miss it in the bulb catalogue. It's certainly worth searching out because it's not difficult to grow from tubers and the enormous, trumpet flowers in various velvety colours are supreme.

Start off the tubers in February, making sure they are the right way up. If you find it difficult to decide, put them in a bag of moist peat in a warm spot until they sprout a shoot. Then pot on, leaving the top of the corm just proud of the surface of the compost.

Put them in bright but indirect sunlight and water when the top of the compost feels just moist. Feed with the high potash fertiliser every two weeks. Maintain humidity by standing the plant over water but don't spray or you'll mark the leaves and flowers.

After flowering, water can gradually be withdrawn and feeding stopped. When the foliage dies down, store the tuber dry until the following February, when it can be started into growth again.

After a few years the tubers may become too big. They can then be cut in half with a live bud on either side.

Hypoestes (Polka-Dot Plant)
The old garden herbaceous plant has come a long way. New hybrids grown as houseplants are close cousins but are much more exotic. The leaves are spotted and splashed with pink, making it an ideal small plant for mixing with others in a planted arrangement.

They can easily be raised from seed sown at any time, but preferably in the spring, and they will also root readily from stem cuttings taken in June.

Put the plants in a sunny window and spray them regularly with water. Feed every two weeks in the summer with the general fertiliser. Keep pinching out the tips of the shoots, to stop the plants becoming straggly. In the winter, reduce watering and stop feeding.

Kalanchoe blossfeldiana
A succulent plant sporting a mass of brilliantly coloured flowers in winter.

They are easily raised from seed sown in March in gentle heat. Pot them into $3\frac{1}{2}$in. (9cm.) pots when the seedlings are big enough to handle and put in bright, indirect sunlight. Water when the top of the compost feels dry and feed once every three weeks with the high potash feed.

After flowering, the plants are best discarded, though they can be brought into flower again following the same light-and-dark treatment as poinsettias (see *Euphorbia*).

Maranta (Prayer Plant)

The beautifully marked leaves fold together at night – hence the common name. The bottoms of the leaves are covered in red hairs and are also very attractive.

They can be divided at repotting time, but this does tend to spoil the shape of the original plant.

Give the plants a bright spot but out of direct sunlight and stand them on a water-filled tray of pebbles to maintain humidity. They'll welcome a regular spray with water too. Water when the top of the compost feels just moist and feed with the general fertiliser every fortnight. In the winter, reduce watering and stop feeding.

Monstera deliciosa (Swiss Cheese Plant)

A great favourite and with good reason: it's not difficult to grow, but it has the one disadvantage of getting a bit unruly.

It will root from stem cuttings taken in June or it can be raised quite successfully from seed sown in June/July in a temperature of 18–21 °C (65–70 °F). Pot them into $3\frac{1}{2}$in. (9cm.) pots when the seedlings are big enough and pot on progressively when the roots fill the pot. Put in bright, indirect sunlight. In poor light, there will be less leaves and less of the attractive splitting of the foliage. Water when the top of the compost feels dry and feed with the general fertiliser every two weeks. In the winter, stop feeding and reduce the watering.

Peperomia

There are several species of this compact little foliage plant, giving a wide permutation of markings. Some leaves are variegated green and yellow while others are curiously puckered and veined.

They'll root readily from stem cuttings in June and should be potted into 3in. (7.5cm.) pots and repotted as required. Don't overpot them because they don't have a very vigorous root system. Put them in good indirect sunlight and stand over water in a tray of pebbles. Water

Above left: *Kalanchoe* 'Pueblo'

Below left: *Hypoestes taeniata*

Above: *Monstera*

Below: *Philodendron erubescens* 'Emerald Queen'

Opposite: Gloxinia (*Sinningia*)

when the top of the compost feels dry and feed once a fortnight with the general fertiliser. In the winter, reduce watering and stop feeding.

Philodendron

There are several types of *Philodendron* with a variety of leaf shapes and habits. Some such as the heart-leaf philodendron (*P. scandens*) are twining plants and are best grown up a support or used to trail from a hanging basket. *P. erubescens* is an erect-growing form, and there are a number of modern varieties of it, with reddish or bright green foliage.

Tip cuttings will root readily provided they have a little bottom heat, or plants that have deteriorated can be air layered. Put them in a semi-shaded spot with more light for the variegated types. Water when the top of the compost feels just moist and feed every fortnight with the general fertiliser. In the winter, reduce watering and stop feeding.

Saintpaulia (African Violet)

This is the most popular of all flowering houseplants. But so much mystery and magic has sprung up around their cultivation that it's often thought that they're difficult. They're not.

Plants can be raised from seed sown in spring or early summer. The seed is left uncovered and put into a polythene bag in full light. Try to arrange a temperature of 21–24°C (70–75°F). Alternatively, they can very easily be propagated from leaf cuttings rooted in water or compost.

Pot new plants into 3–3½in. (7.5–9cm.) pots and put them in good light but not direct sunlight. Water very carefully either from above, avoiding wetting the leaves, or by immersion. Avoid over-watering but don't let them dry out if possible – though that's better than the other extreme.

Spray with hot water regularly and stand the pots on gravel in a water-filled tray. Feed once a fortnight with the high potash fertiliser or preferably with a special Saintpaulia feed available from garden centres.

In the winter, reduce watering and do not feed.

Scindapsus (Devil's Ivy)

A fine climber with heart-shaped leaves of green or variegated green and yellow or cream.

It can be propagated by taking stem cuttings in June either in water or in compost. Put the plants in a semi-shaded position, standing the pots on pebbles in a water-filled tray. Water when the top of the compost feels just moist and feed with the general fertiliser every fortnight.

To encourage bushy growth, pinch out the growing tips regularly or prune back more drastically if the plant gets out of hand. Those tips can all be used for cuttings. In the winter, water when the compost feels dry and move the plants to full light.

Stephanotis (Madagascar Jasmine)

An evergreen climber with the most superb waxy white flowers that will fill your room with fragrance.

It can be grown from stem cuttings in June but they're not easy, so take plenty. Pot the plants into small pots but pot on progressively as they fill the containers. They are fairly vigorous climbers so it's best to train them round a wire hoop, as for jasmine.

Stephanotis prefers a light position out of direct sunshine and a humid atmosphere, so stand the pot on wet pebbles. Water when the top of the compost feels just moist and feed with the high potash fertiliser every fortnight. In the winter, put it on a sunny windowsill out of draughts and reduce watering.

Picture Credits
The publishers would like to thank the following for the use of their photographs on the pages listed. Flower Council of Holland: pages 11, 15, 18, 31 (left), 51, 62, 63, 67, 86, 87 (above, centre and right), 90 (above and right), 91, 94 (below left and above), 95, 98 (right), 99, 102 (right), 103, 106 (above and below), 110, 111 (left), 114, 115, 118, 119, 122, 123. Harry Smith Horticultural Photographic Collection: pages 14, 19, 22, 26, 27, 31 (above), 70, 71, 74, 75, 78, 79, 82, 83, 87 (left), 94 (above left), 102 (below), 107, 111 (above). Buralls of Wisbech: pages 31 (below), 102 (above). Geest: pages 90 (below), 98 (above), 106 (right).

INDEX
Italic figures refer to illustrations